WORDS OF HOPE
AND HEALING FROM
THE DIRECTORS OF
GEORGIA'S CHILDREN'S
ADVOCACY CENTERS

To Mimi —
Thank you
so much for
what you've
done for.
CACGA!
Best.
(signature)

WORDS OF HOPE AND HEALING FROM THE DIRECTORS OF GEORGIA'S CHILDREN'S ADVOCACY CENTERS

Encouragement and Empowerment
for Survivors of Child Abuse

CHILDREN'S ADVOCACY CENTERS OF GEORGIA

To order additional copies of this book, contact:
Xlibris
1-888-795-4274
www.Xlibris.com
Orders@Xlibris.com
731539

TABLE OF CONTENTS

For the children. We stand by your side.

The Children's Advocacy Centers of Georgia is supported by its sponsoring agency, the Georgia Department of Human Services – Division of Family and Children Services. Thank you!

ABOUT THIS BOOK

We remember the children long after we serve them at our children's advocacy centers. The idea for this book developed for that reason.

Our impact on children is usually measured by how we serve them at our CACs. Through our services, we strive to provide them with hope and healing so that their young lives will continue to hold promise for the future.

The Children's Advocacy Centers of Georgia consists of forty-six CACs all across the state. At a recent directors' meeting, the question was asked: *How often do you think about the children after they leave your CAC?*

A unanimous *all the time* was the response.

We discussed that all of our professionals who work within a children's advocacy center try to be a positive influence on the children while they are in our care. But wouldn't it be wonderful if we could expand this positive influence to children after they leave our CACs?

And so, an idea followed: *Let's write a book, and why don't you, directors, each write a chapter? During the time the children are at your center, they are embraced by your team through a variety of services. But what happens after they leave your center? We know that a child is not "a case," but a person. Do you think that they have questions about their future?*

In this book, our directors have written about hope, encouragement, and empowerment. They have imagined through their writings what it would be like sitting with a child and non-offending caregiver on their final day at the CAC when a child asks: *What now? What is my life going to be like? What happens to kids like me who've had things like this happen to them? How can I be successful? How can I trust? How can I love? Who cares about me?* Or any number of the many questions that have been asked by children over the years.

For the children: We hope that this book provides as much hope to you as you have provided to us by showing us your courage and strength. We will always stand with you.

Andrew Agatston
CEO/General Counsel
Children's Advocacy Centers of Georgia

FIRST FOREWORD

by Chris Newlin

Child abuse is a serious issue. I kind of knew this as a kid, and I sure know it now as an adult. I have worked in the child abuse field for almost thirty years, and I have seen incredibly significant changes and improvements in our nation's response to child abuse over this time.

I started my career working in a residential treatment center for adolescents, and although I was taught almost nothing about child abuse, I quickly realized that every single adolescent in our program had experienced significant trauma in their lives. I wondered, "Why did my college and graduate school not prepare me for this? What can I do to help these kids?" I did my best, but these were the early days. We didn't really have meaningful programs to respond to the needs of children. We didn't have quality investigations to determine what has happened to these kids, to provide an effective response, and to hold offenders accountable.

This was very frustrating. I felt powerless and could only imagine how powerless the adolescents in the program were feeling. I then transitioned to working at a children's hospital, providing therapy for families impacted by child sexual abuse and conducting research to assess the psychophysiological impacts of child abuse on children. It was during this time that I met someone who would change my life forever.

It was 1992, and Susie (not her real name) was an inspirational thirteen-year-old girl who would seem to have everything going for her. She was articulate, athletic, attractive, outgoing. She had everything going for her, but, she had also been sexually abused by her father on two occasions.

Her father was not someone who you would ever expect to do something like this. He was gainfully employed, intelligent, very involved in his family and community, but he did some terrible things. There was no Child Advocacy Center (CAC) for Susie when she disclosed what he had done. She was interviewed by multiple people from Child Protective Services and Law Enforcement, and the investigation lingered, holding Susie, her siblings, her mother, and the community hostage. Her father was ultimately arrested, and I was seeing Susie in therapy. One day, while we were talking (I remember it like it was yesterday), she looked at me and said, "If I had it to do all over again, I wish I had not told about what he did. What me and my family have been through was worse than what my dad did to me."

I was stunned and did my best to respond to Susie while I had a myriad of thoughts running through my head . . . "How can the system's response have been worse than your father sexually abusing you? What will this mean if one of your friends confides in you that he/she was sexually abused? What will this mean if you have a child of your own one day and suspect child sexual abuse?" Susie went on to explain her feelings about the response to her disclosure, and quite honestly, I could not fault her for feeling the way she did. I am sure she was not alone in feeling this way. In fact, over the years, I have met so many mothers and fathers of children seen at CACs who have shared their stories of child sexual abuse and the poor response, if any, they experienced at the time.

> "I felt compelled by Susie to do something . . . anything, to make a difference for other children experiencing child abuse. It is great that we can provide therapy, but if children are harmed by the initial response to their disclosures of child abuse that should be more sensitive and responsive to their needs, there is no way they will ever make it to therapy."

I felt compelled by Susie to do something . . . anything, to make a difference for other children experiencing child abuse. It is great that we can provide therapy, but if children are harmed by the initial response to their disclosures of child abuse that should be more sensitive and responsive to their needs, there is no way they will ever make it to therapy.

Little did I know that other professionals were experiencing the same thing. One particular individual was Bud Cramer, the District Attorney in Madison County, Alabama (Huntsville). He was frustrated with the inability of his office to effectively prosecute child abuse cases because the courageous victims who came forward were simply tired of telling their story repeatedly and were also feeling the same way as Susie. The "system" that was supposed to serve them was actually causing them additional trauma. Bud Cramer was in a position to do something about it—he was the elected district attorney. He looked around the country to see what other people were doing, and he found nothing but similar frustrations and circumstances. He challenged the numerous professionals responsible for responding to child abuse to completely change their response to child abuse. Bud had two primary tenets on which the entire CAC model is built:

1. The only way we can successfully respond to child abuse is to fully engage the numerous professionals responding to this issue—law enforcement, child protective services, prosecutors, victim advocates, mental health, and medical professionals.
2. This "system" should not cause additional trauma for the child but actually help the child and improve the ability to hold those who abuse children accountable.

Bud Cramer recognized that the traditional criminal justice and child protection systems were not achieving the desired outcomes and a new model was needed. Instead of children (and families) having to go to numerous agencies and talk to numerous individuals about the same highly sensitive information over and over, in settings that were overwhelming and intimidating, why not have all of the professionals responsible for responding to child abuse do so in a child-friendly environment? Duh . . . common sense is a great thing, and it has turned out to be an extraordinary thing.

There are now more than 850 CACs in the United States that served more than 320,000 children in 2015 alone. There are CACs operating in twenty-six countries throughout the world as they see the tremendous value in providing a more victim-friendly, victim-centered approach. This is not about law enforcement, child protective services, prosecutors, victim advocates, mental health professionals, and medical professionals getting what they need. It is about those who have experienced abuse getting what they need from these professionals.

Child abuse should not become the organizing principle of anyone's life. It is, for countless individuals, part of the human experience. However, if bad things happen, they should not dictate our entire future. People say things that are not true: "Her/His life is ruined. He/she will never be the same. He/she will never get over this." We all have negative things that happen in our lives, but as long as we fall back on, or support the thought that these issues are the cause for any problems we have, then we are not taking control of our lives. We may have lots of strong feelings about what happened, but it does not define who we are.

It is my sincere hope that if you are reading this foreword, then all of this makes perfect sense to you. Please know that I, and Bud Cramer, stand by your side in this journey, and there are countless more dedicated professionals who are also standing beside you. We will not leave you. We will do our best for you, and if you feel we are not, then you should say something. It was that courage to "say something" that started this whole journey, for both you and the professionals working with you now.

Chris Newlin is the executive director of the National Children's Advocacy Center in Huntsville, Alabama.

SECOND FOREWORD

by Nancy Chandler

If you are reading this book or any of the chapters, you have probably just gone through hearing the awful news that your child, or the child for whom you provide care, has been the victim of abuse. Hearing those words, while terrifying and disheartening, can also be the time when you begin the road to health and to healing. While the abuse is very personal to you and you probably feel like no one can understand how you are truly feeling, take heart in knowing that hundreds of thousands of others have walked in your footsteps. While every road is different, ultimately you want the same that all caring adults want in this situation, to know that your child will receive all the care possible and that the help they receive will place them on the road to healing from the abuse and having a strong, healthy, productive life.

Since you are reading this book, it probably also means that you have been provided services by a Children's Advocacy Center. If so, you are very fortunate. Prior to 1985, the system designed to help children often revictimized children through the disconnected and unskilled attempts at service. In 1985 the first forward thinking comprehensive approach was taken to bring all of the members of the multidisciplinary team working in the field of child abuse together. The effort revolutionized the work of providing coordinated services to child victims. Rather than each member

> *"At the heart of the work of supporting children and their families is the multidisciplinary team."*

of the team (law enforcement, child protective services, medical, mental health, and prosecution) each having to interview the child and ask the same questions over and over, a new approach was founded. For the first time, one trained interviewer was tasked with asking the questions that all of the team members needed to do their job. Children could begin to feel a sense of safety in speaking to one person, trained to help the child talk of their experiences in their own words. Equally important was that the process was designed to ensure that the questions were not leading the child on, but rather, focused on elucidating the truth from the child as to what did or did not happen. The child was allowed to tell their information in their own way and in their own time.

Central to this work was that the other members of the team were then able to use the information gained during the interview to complete their own further investigation of the abuse report. In that way, trained law enforcement officers could do the work they were trained to do: determine if a crime has been committed and if so, to determine the offender and present that information to the District Attorney/State Attorney. Child welfare staff could focus on what they do best: determine if the child is safe from further harm and if not, to find other ways to protect the child. The medical profession was able to take the time to learn whether or not the child had been physically harmed, and if so, to begin immediate treatment and to reassure the child about their body. Ultimately, the decision to charge someone with abuse would rest with the District Attorney, but this decision could be based on the best efforts and information presented by the full complement of the team.

In this way, the services that are provided to children have grown and expanded. Medical staff has more rigorous training in diagnosing and treating abuse and the mental health community has learned to work with trauma in a focused, professional manner. The advent of trauma-focused therapy saw that children who had been harmed could carry that trauma into their adulthood without proper intervention. The profession learned that many of the children who came through the doors of a Children's Advocacy Center has suffered other trauma in their lives, and that the opportunity to take the time to work through the issues of trauma could have a major positive and long lasting impact on the child and family.

At the heart of the work of supporting children and their families is the multidisciplinary team. The first team members that the child and family will meet are usually the staff of the Children's Advocacy Center. Whether the first person is a client services coordinator, director of the center, the forensic interviewer or the family advocate, their goal is the same—to make certain that the needs of the child and family are fully understood and that the appropriate services are provided.

The forensic interviewer is the person who has received extensive, specific training in interviewing children in a manner that is not hostile or threatening but rather engaging. The interviewer will work to build rapport with the child before digging into the tough questions that need to be answered. One goal of the interviewer is that having shared the details of the abuse, the child will feel a sense of shared burden and of not having to hold on to the details of the abuse in secret and alone. At the same time, the interviewer will be looking to see if there are "alternative hypotheses" that would explain the situation that the child is recalling with an eye to seeing if something other than an abusive experience occurred. This is for the benefit of the child as well as for the gathering of information for the team. It is hoped that the interviewer will be able to get sufficient information from the child that only one interview is necessary, but sometimes that isn't the case, particularly for very young children, children with limited language skills, or children who have been quite traumatized.

After the interview is concluded, the family usually meets with law enforcement, child protective services, the interviewer, and a victim advocate to determine the next steps to be taken. This is often the most difficult meeting for parents as they learn the facts of the case from the professionals involved. Every parent hopes that their child was not abused, and often this meeting is when they learn that their child has, in fact, been hurt. This meeting sets the stage for the work ahead, and parents need to know that the professionals with whom they meet are there to make sure that the child is not further harmed and that the child will be protected going into the future.

After the plan is discussed, staff of the Child Advocacy Center will usually make a referral for follow-up therapy for the child and the family members.

This therapy may occur on-site at the Child Advocacy Center or through referral to an outside agency or outside therapist. The most important thing to know is that the person to whom the child and family is referred has significant training in trauma-informed therapy, the most efficient and highly regarded type of therapy dealing with children who have been victimized. In addition, the therapist will work with the family to make sure that there is not a financial burden placed on the family by attending to therapy.

Also occurring will be a referral to a family advocate whose job is to make sure that the child and family understand what will happen in the days, weeks, and sometimes even years to come as the case against the offender is resolved. This family advocate knows the steps ahead and is there to help each member of the family receive the support that they need. If there are other referrals to be made for transportation, assistance with housing, or with other needs, the advocate can step in to provide this help. The family advocates are there for the long run, to answer questions, explain the process, and to be with the child and family if and when the case goes to court.

Just as in the referral to therapy, there will probably be a referral for the child to be seen by a medical professional. This medical professional may be a doctor or a nurse, but all medical professionals working with the Child Advocacy Center have had extensive training in recognizing the signs of abuse and in helping children and family members work through any issues that arise during the course of the examination. They are there to see if there are any medical issues that need to be addressed and to make recommendations for any follow up appointments or medication if needed.

The most important take away for parents or caregivers, however, is that they have a team to help them through the difficult days ahead. If your child was abused, they are there to make sure that the offender is held accountable and that the child is safe from further harm. While it may be a little overwhelming and scary to suddenly have all of these "official" people involved in your and your child's life, take heart in knowing that these professionals have all been trained to do this specific work. Whatever their profession, the individuals working within a children's advocacy center either on staff or as team members, take this work very seriously and they take the work of protecting children as their duty. While everyone would wish that abuse never happened, when it does, the best hope is that the child and family are able to access the services of a Children's Advocacy Center, the place where the needs of the child come first.

Nancy Chandler was the executive director of the National Children's Alliance in Washington D.C. from 1994 to 2007. Prior to that, she was the founding executive director of the Memphis Children's Advocacy Center in Memphis, Tennessee. Most recently, she retired as CEO of the Georgia Center for Child Advocacy in Atlanta, Georgia.

THIRD FOREWORD

by "Jane Doe," a mother whose child was served at a children's advocacy center

My eyes are stinging with tears that want to flow, my heart is in my throat and my stomach . . . well, I am not sure how to describe how it is feeling.

I open the car door and try to appear casual and calm while grabbing my four-year-old child's hand. I even try to seem lighthearted and silly. Realizing the old adage about laughing or crying as a reaction to the same event is true, we walk across the parking lot to what appears to be the main entrance. A buzzer loomed. I meekly say who I am and why I am there. I also notice a police station connected to the building. Oh my God, what is happening? A kind voice answers the buzzer, and the door clicks open. My husband, child, and I walk into a world we know nothing about. Kindness and compassion flow on to us as we are welcomed inside. My child is offered a stuffed bear or a blanket as a source of comfort. A blanket is chosen. My heart starts pounding harder and faster when I see the hand-sewn label on the blanket, "Project Linus." My fears are confirmed. Something awful has happened and it happened to my child.

> *"My child is offered a stuffed bear or a blanket as a source of comfort. A blanket is chosen. My heart starts pounding harder and faster when I see the hand-sewn label on the blanket, "Project Linus."*

Before the day my husband, child, and I walked into the children's advocacy center, we were a very typical family. There were five of us—me, my husband, and our three children. Okay, there were six of us, if you include our dachshund. We lived in a large city. That meant my husband had a long commute for work and I stayed home taking care of our children. I also worked from home which allowed me to arrange my work hours around preschool carpool, playgroups, and the occasional sick child. How did such a normal family end up in crisis and walking into a children's advocacy center? You may likely guessed by now that my child was sexually abused. Now he has a new favorite blanket.

"It's my body and it's nobody's body but mine," my child is singing from the back seat. "Stop!" his siblings are yelling with hands over their ears. It's a song that was taught in his group therapy session at the CAC; a song with words to reinforce the lessons about body safety. We are on our way home, and I asked my child how it had gone in class that day. That's when the song broke out which lasted almost until we got to McDonald's where we stopped for dinner.

When a cup flies across the table toward his older sibling, I know that it was not all fun and games at the CAC today. During the lesson on body safety, my child has figured out that the touching was wrong. This realization caused a fit which resulted in the drink going all over his sibling and the table. This was an ugly scene, but it needed to happen in order for my child to process, understand, and cross over to the other side of the abuse with a healthy heart and mind. There were many times like these as my child moved through therapy. We showed our love, and we were patient. This included his siblings, one older and one younger. Our family found strength in honesty and openness. We were all there to support each other.

The professionals at the CAC continually encouraged my husband and me with the knowledge that a child who receives therapy along with love and support at home, will thrive and be okay. That's what we wanted for our child, for our child to be okay. Both individual and group therapy continued regularly for several months after we found out about the abuse. At the conclusion of his therapy, we were told that the door is always open and if we needed additional support later on—weeks, months, years, we could always call. That sounded nice, but the day I walked out the door was a very difficult day for me. I felt like the blanket of comfort and support that the CAC provided had just been yanked off.

A long period later and after we had made progress toward putting the abuse behind us, the criminal trial began. It was time to test the CAC's words that the door was always open. I could feel the familiar blanket of kindness being placed on me as soon as the phone was answered. My child's therapist was there to help him understand the process of testifying and to help ease the pain of the subject of his abuse being brought up again. So, at six years old, my child was able to sit in that big chair in the front of the courtroom and answer questions. My child is my hero with super powers; I am not sure where they came from. The support of our CAC definitely helped, but there were so many aspects of the criminal case that were out of their control and ours—delays, multiple changes in representation, changing prosecution strategy, and many more delays. Keeping a normal routine through it all helped as did trying to be lighthearted when the trial-related activities came up. Parenting a super hero witness requires putting on your own cape and providing a lot of love and support.

That was several years ago. I am relieved to tell you that my child is happy and well-adjusted, likes sports, and has a messy room. My child is okay and our family is back to normal. I don't think about the abuse my child suffered on a daily basis nor see my child through a victim filter. I don't worry that each and every issue that comes up is the result of abuse. I just love my child who loves back.

Until today, when I sat down to write this foreword, my child's Project Linus blanket sat in the bedroom closet. It sat there ready to be pulled out for comfort just as the CAC sits ready if I need to call, and just as your child advocacy center will be there for you too. Now, I look at his blanket on my desk next to my notes. I hope that one day these notes in the form of a foreword and the words from many dedicated child advocates that follow will serve as a source of hope and healing for you and your family on your journey to back to normal.

The writer is a mother of a child, a super hero child, who received services at a children's advocacy center.

———

CHAPTER 1

The Eclectic Chairs and the Children Who Sit There

We were so proud of our eclectic cool chairs bought at the Habitat Store. They were perfect for all ages with tons of colors, sequins, embroidery, and whimsy. Everyone complimented those chairs when we brought them into the CAC. Then came the nervous hands . . .

As we sit and talk, your fingers desperately pull at the strings looking for a place to call their own. Those tiny nails pick at the sequins until they pop off, and you then have an object to focus on instead of the discussion of brutality. Your hand brushes back and forth at a fevered pace on one side of the chair as you draw pictures of your abuser with the other, leaving fragments of embroidered flowers in their path. I'm taking note, not because of worry over the chairs, but needing to listen to you with my eyes as well as my ears. You say so much as you shred that chair.

You tell me how embarrassed you are about what you had no control over, yet you continue to show grace and composure despite being videotaped through your disclosure. You lower your eyes because you think

> *"You are so smart. You make better interviewers than we are so often. You love to catch us off guard and ask us questions about our own children, our favorite colors, and where do we live. Sometimes, you really like to ask those questions that make our hearts skip a beat: Have you lost someone you love? Will I ever be able to trust anyone again? What happens next?"*

you should have fought off your offender, not knowing how brilliant you were for acting exactly as you did and surviving. You provide details and descriptions that most adults can't repeat in hushed tones, much less in slow steady voices when asked to speak up for my "old ears." You don't know it, but you are so brave as you shred that chair.

When you leave the interview room, your world is so often a very different place. You probably held on to your secrets a lot longer than you wanted to, to avoid changing the fabric of your family and your life. What a cruel responsibility was placed on you. Whether you were told to keep a secret or whether you *just knew* you were supposed to, the person that took advantage of you now must bear the burden of that secret. It is no longer yours to carry. You belong to a lionhearted club now. The small percentage of children abused who tell while still in childhood.

We will follow your progress whether you know it or not. There is an entire team of people that will follow your "case" until you go to court. We know court scares you and your family. Sometimes the adults don't understand why court is such an issue and causes so much fear since you faced so much fear alone in the dark and survived. We know it is because it is all being shown for what it truly is in the light and that can be even more terrifying. It is not possible to pretend to be asleep when sitting in a witness chair explaining to a room full of people what you may never have intended to tell at all.

You are so smart. You make better interviewers than we are so often. You love to catch us off guard and ask us questions about our own children, our favorite colors, and where do we live. Sometimes, you really like to ask those questions that make our hearts skip a beat: Have you lost someone you love? Will I ever be able to trust anyone again? What happens next? We often have to answer questions with questions because that is what we are trained to do. But we want to answer your questions with more than a question more than you know.

Yes, I've lost someone I love. That pain is awful and at first is very hard to handle. Every single day you will find memories in the recesses of your mind of that person that make you remember the good times with them, make you smile and eventually you find the laughter you had with them. Never forget them. Hold them in the most special part of your heart and honor them by living the best possible life you can. Honor someone you've loved and lost by taking care of yourself and sharing that love with those that need it.

What happens next? That might be the best question ever posed. If we answer it honestly, we would say, we don't know. There are too many variables. We often have a good idea, but there is never a guarantee. There will be so many factors that control where you will go, who you will be with, how safe you will be, whether or not you will receive counseling . . . the list feels infinite sometimes. Just know that the Children's Advocacy Center is going to work extremely hard to make sure all the right people come together from all the right places to do the best work possible on your behalf. We don't know what your immediate next years are like privately. Only you really know how that feels. Sometimes we get the pleasure of seeing you and hearing for ourselves how you have been doing over the years. You may not be able to control all of the circumstances and others in your life. You do have control over your thoughts, your heart, and your future. Find your focus there when times are tough.

Yes, you will be able to trust. The events in your life have shaped and molded your views of the world in a way others may not understand. Be a student of your life. Study the patterns of those that behaved poorly and did not have your best interest at heart, and avoid relationships with people that act in a similar fashion. You have extra "Spidey sense," but do not let it make you so jaded that you miss out on the beauty of relationships with good people. Always listen to your "uh-oh" feelings, *let go and live*. Susan Jeffers said, "Ships are safe in harbors, but that's not what ships are built for." You can spend the rest of your life not trusting other people and be "safe," but you are built for far better things. Don't let your abuser keep you in harbor for one second.

There is a question that I'm not sure I've ever been asked aloud in my career, but it needs answering. How do I forgive myself? You may find yourself at some point doing things you know are not good for you. You may be in relationships with someone or with people that you know are not right.

You may be behaving poorly at home, at school, or in public. You may be using drugs or alcohol. You may be harming yourself. You may be harming other people. Sometimes these behaviors are cries for help. Sometimes these behaviors are signs of self-hatred. Sometimes victims haven't made it into being survivors yet. If you find yourself here, it could be that you may be angry at the system, the abuser, or even yourself. You were taught at some point that it was okay to abuse you. If you are in this place right now, take a deep breath and reach out for help. You are not broken. You are not less than. We all make mistakes. Every day that you wake up is a new day to forgive yourself and start over. If you realize anger is an issue, let others who care about you help you with it. Anger is fuel for self-abuse.

Back to those shredded chairs. It has been four years since we bought our new chairs. They have definitely been broken in. The interesting thing is, when we have visitors, they *still* complement our chairs. It is one of the first things people notice. They do not notice the pulled strings, missing sequins, unraveled embroidery, and tears on the sides. It could be because the chair patterns are so attractive, complex, busy, and eclectic, just like you. It could be partly because although you shred our chairs, you instinctively try to weave back some of the strings you notice pulled or pull together torn spots when you first sit down. Sometimes it feels like you are paying homage to the last child that sat in that same spot. You are literally mending the anxiety of the previous inhabitant. The only people that notice the worn spots on the shredded chairs are the ones that have traveled the same road.

When you visit us, we see not only your worry, fear, or anxiety. We see your intelligence, your humor, your bravery, your talent, and your perseverance. Whether you are three or sixteen, boy or girl, big or little, you are all lionhearted. It is an honor to sit in those shredded chairs with you.

Amy Boney is the executive director of the Lighthouse Children's Advocacy Center in Americus, Georgia.

CHAPTER 2

Choose Today

The building comes into view and you laugh to yourself because you have passed this place countless times—going to a friend's house, going to school, going home. The laughter stops because the thought of home reminds you of "The Thing," and there is nothing funny about "The Thing." You quickly realize that this building will never be just another bland landmark in the scenes of your everyday life. You take a deep breath as the car comes to a stop and this thought pops into your mind, "I just won't go inside. No one can make me. I will just sit here and all the people who want me to do this will just have to figure it out themselves. I have done enough. I'm not going inside." Then you look to your left and a figure catches your eye. It's your little sister and you know that you will go inside. For her. You open the car door, take a deep breath, and put on the mask that has gotten you through so many things before, "Let's just get this over with." A comment to hide your fear and a prayer that maybe this time it really will be over.

A flurry of activity surrounds you, and you realize no one is looking at you like you have grown two heads. A kind face asks if you need anything and you shake your head

> *"Something we tell every caregiver we encounter is that their belief and support of their child is the most important factor in the child's healing process. A child needs to know that the people in charge of keeping them safe will do just that, no matter the cost. We recognize that for some families there is a cost, a price to pay, but nothing is more important than the safety and well-being of a child."*

as your sister lunges for the toys on the ground. It's a blur and time does that funny thing where it moves so fast and not at all. Before you know it, a stranger is introducing herself and saying it's time to talk. A squeeze of your loved one's hand for courage and you find yourself following this person; undecided as to whether or not they will be the one to bear the secret you have held for so long.

No two children are the same; they all come in with unique needs, experiences, and perspectives of whatever it is they have been through. However, every child we encounter has one thing in common regardless of what they have experienced; they all reach the point where they have to make a choice. This point, this place in time, can be imagined as something like a fork in the road, but instead of seeing just two clear paths, picture both paths with their own set of obstacles, off-shooting branches, and difficulties. Neither path is safe; neither is without risk and even *considering* either path requires a substantial amount of courage. If you were to take all of these factors away, remove the fear and confusion, and look at this decision a child must make in its simplest form, you would be left with the question, will I tell? If this feels like a heavy responsibility for a child to have, it is. We ask children to hold the weight of their experiences and then share them, openly and completely, oftentimes with a complete stranger and then to trust that some inexplicable system will keep them safe. That is courage in action.

To look across the table, into a child's eyes and ask them hard, sometimes uncomfortable questions is not a brave thing. It is a necessary thing that we do as trained professionals, equipped with the skills needed to move through this kind of conversation. For the child, however, there is no training, no handbook, no past experience to be drawn on to help them know what to do or to say. For the child it is a leap of faith and a firm grip on the belief that everything will be okay.

You walk down a hallway and then another and then into room that looks like it was forgotten when they decorated the place. You sit across from the stranger, and as time goes on they become less of a stranger and more of the person that you will always associate with this experience. You talk about yourself: where you go to school, what you like to do for fun, and instead of feeling like a criminal being interrogated for information you feel like . . . yourself. There is still something there. That knot that feels like it has taken up permanent residence in your stomach. It is easy to sit here and tell them all about acing the science test and watching your sister play with her new puppy. You could do this all day, but then it comes down to "The Thing." Why doesn't it just go away? It would be so simple to keep up this conversation; to talk about everything and nothing until the nice people decide there isn't anything to know after all.

The voices start in your mind. "If you tell, no one will believe you," "It's our little secret, and good kids don't tell secrets," "Your mom wouldn't love you anymore if she knew," "Don't worry, this is what is supposed to happen," "You deserve this," "It's your fault." The thoughts swirl and tumble through your mind and you know if it isn't today, if it isn't now, it will be never. You see in your mind all of the things you want in life: to have friends, to maybe go to college, to see the Grand Canyon, to make it to tomorrow. Suddenly those things, that life, is so important, so necessary, that the voices that have kept you quiet for so long are muffled and then stomped out. A question rings through the chaos, a simple question, "How come you are here today?"

You meet the stranger's eyes, take a deep breath, and start to speak.

There is a moment during your time with a child where you see their mind working, their heart deciding which way to go. In that moment there is nothing that we can do to help the child choose outside of just being there. We hope that everything we have said or done conveys to the child that we are just there to listen, but ultimately it comes down to them. This is where that act of bravery really comes into play because we generally know what it means for a child to make the choice to tell. In some situations, it might mean that the child is removed from their home, their community, and placed somewhere deemed safer. For others, it might be that the child can stay in their home but their family is forever changed and once-secure relationships now need mending. For all children it means confronting the situation head-on and saying, "This won't control me anymore."

An unexpected feeling washes over you and it takes a few minutes before you can put it into words. Relief. You feel relieved. The ever-present knot seems to have taken a vacation and you want to laugh with this new feeling but that would seem very out of place and strange. You told some parts, so many parts that you never thought you would tell. You don't recognize it yet, but you left out the worst time. No one could handle hearing about that, but none of that matters right now. You did it. You know things will change now, they have to. Your home will feel safe again, and that thought alone is enough to put a smile on your face.

As you sit in the car and drive away from the building and your loved one tells you, "I am so proud of you," you seriously think you might cry, and suddenly it all feels like too much. The good, the bad, and the unimaginable fill your mind and you can't believe that stupid knot is back. You look out the window and force yourself to pull it together. Today is a day you never thought would come and nothing is going to ruin it. "The Thing" is over.

For so many the telling is only step one. This is only the first part of healing, because even when you extract the bullet the wound remains. For some children what once was "normal" is now a source of grief and pain to everyone around them, and taking care of that pain becomes the most important thing. Most children are acutely aware of the emotions of those they love and can feel responsible for caring for those who are supposed to be caring for them. For a child who has experienced something so scary, a trauma, their bodies cannot believe it is okay to feel safe in a place that was once so unsafe. Their minds continue to try to protect them with unnecessary feelings of anxiety and worrying thoughts. The nightmare seems to continue to control them even though the monster is gone. We know this is going to happen for many children. We know that even if they are not talking about what happened, they are most likely thinking about it, and we are hopeful that these children will make another brave and difficult choice—the choice to allow someone else in, to trust another stranger with their thoughts and emotions; the choice to heal and truly move on.

You feel it all too much now. The moments where you feel okay only make the hard moments harder and you need a way out. You are so lucky to have a loved one that notices, one that sees your pain and wants better for you. But they are asking the impossible of you again, and you wonder why that building wants so much from you. The stranger you meet this time is a different one, a little younger, a lot peppier. You tell her more about yourself and wonder if at the end of all of this there will be anything left for you to keep, just for you to know. You begin to learn more about what you experienced. You learn just how often it happens and some reasons why. It's strange though, your counselor doesn't mention anything about things you could've done to stop it or some reasons why it's your fault. The thought doesn't even seem to cross her mind even though you can't get it out of yours. You begin to wonder if maybe all of those things they said about it being your fault were even true, but how could it not be true . . . in your mind you believe that you let it go on for so long.

As you learn more and more you find yourself relating to the experiences your counselor describes. When she tells you that a lot of kids feel damaged or broken you softly whisper, "Yeah, me too." That's all you're ready to say for now and that seems okay. She calls what happened to you by its name; she refuses to call it "The Thing" and at first it makes your skin crawl. Over time however, hearing the name becomes normal and you start to use it too. She tells you and your loved one that it is always up to you if you want to come to counseling. No one is forcing you. It is your choice. Sometimes it is the last thing you want to do after a long day at school, but every week you find yourself reminding your loved one that it's time to go and you make your way to that building once again.

Something we tell every caregiver we encounter is that their belief and support of their child is the most important factor in the child's healing process. A child needs to know that the people in charge of keeping them safe will do just that, no matter the cost. We recognize that for some families there is a cost, a price to pay, but nothing is more important than the safety and well-being of a child. Caregivers are often struggling with some of the same feelings and thoughts that their child struggles with. Thoughts like, "I should've done more," "How could I not know?" or "I trusted that person. What does that say about me?" These are thoughts and questions we hear all the time. The feeling of guilt is universal to almost all caregivers. We provide statistics and information learned over time through experience and training. We strive to partner with caregivers as they grow the capacity to understand what their child experienced. At the end of the day, however, it is vital that caregivers remember that at the core of everything their child is still their child. What has happened to their family is not what defines their family, just the same as what happened to their child does not define their child. It is not everything they are. We encourage caregivers to maintain a sense of normalcy, to give their child back the life that someone tried so hard to steal.

Recently, a caregiver shared that as she waited for her child to finish counseling, she noticed another family in the waiting room and she could just tell they were there for the same reason her family had been there so long ago. She felt compassion for that family and wanted, more than anything, to go to them and let them know that it would be okay. She wanted to wrap her arms around that family and tell them that she understood their pain, had felt their pain, and had somehow found a way through to a place of healing.

You hold the piece of paper and steady your trembling hand. You have read this for what feels like a thousand times, and by now the feelings of embarrassment and shame feel like they belong to a different person. You are glad your loved one already knows what you are going to say, that your counselor has been preparing you both for this day. You will share your experience of abuse with your loved one and they will finally know all that you have held inside for so long. There have been so many days, so many nights, when you wished you could talk about it at home but stopped yourself because what if they can't handle it. Well, now you will know for sure, and as you meet your loved ones' eyes they invite you to begin. Your voice comes out clear and steady and you find yourself speaking the details you never thought you would tell, the parts you thought no one could handle. Before you know it you are reading the final words that you wrote just last week, the words it took you so long to believe.

"And I now know it isn't my fault. I did a brave thing by telling and if I could say anything to another kid going through this I will tell them to be strong. I would want them to find someone, anyone they could tell. I would tell them that there are people who care, people who can help them. And one day they will feel happy again."

Page Sanders is the Child Services Program Manager at The Treehouse Children's Advocacy Center in Winder, Georgia.

CHAPTER 3

The Hero

Have you ever asked yourself what makes an individual a "hero?" If you were to look up the word "hero" in the dictionary you would see that it is defined as a person who is admired for courage, outstanding achievements, or noble qualities.

My children and I recently returned from a trip to Universal Studios and Warner Brothers Studio in California. We enjoyed seeing all the different characters we had seen on TV and in the movies. We even got to see some famous sports stars and musicians. One thing that really stuck out in my mind is how we all seem to look at these "famous" movie stars, singers, athletes as "heroes." Millions of dollars are spent every year so that we can get close to these people and gain a glimpse into their everyday lives.

After we returned from our trip, I began to wonder what it means to be a true "hero." Do we consider people heroes because they are rich, good looking, have a good job, drive a fancy car? Are heroes male or female, young or old? When I was growing up, my heroes were people like Superman, Batman, Wonder Woman, and even the police and firefighters I sometimes saw in the streets of the small, southern town in which I

> "Through the years when I think back at my childhood, I remember the happy times and sometimes I think about the bad. Just like you, those scars will always be there on the inside but that does not mean I can't move forward. It doesn't mean YOU can't move forward."

lived. Heroes brought to mind the teachers I saw each day at school and the coaches who spent numerous hours teaching me a love for the game of tennis. My hero was that youth counselor who listened to all the problems of a bunch of teenage girls.

I grew up, like many of you, in what seemed like a happy, stable, and perfect family.

I lived on the golf course of the local country club, was in church every Wednesday and Sunday, and in all of my home photos I had a big smile on my face. Few people, if any, knew what my life was like behind closed doors. Like many of the boys, girls, and parents that come through our local child advocacy center, I kept things "private." I was taught that you don't discuss what goes on at home to your friends or teachers. When the teachers ask where the bruises on your arm came from, make sure you tell them you fell on the trampoline or some kind of story like that.

Dad wasn't always a monster. Sometimes he would play with me and take me places for fun. He even taught me how to ride a bike. Holidays and birthdays were always the worst times though. I would hide his alcohol thinking if he didn't drink I wouldn't get hit. This just made his anger worse. I was often told that I was the reason for his drinking. I didn't know any better so I believed him. I remember praying to the Lord that I could be a better daughter. I didn't want him to hurt me anymore. I wanted all the screaming and yelling to stop. I began to think that his behavior was normal . . . that this happens in everyone's family.

When I first started working with children and families, I would often go home and think about those times as a young child when I felt alone and afraid. I would ask myself why I never told anyone about the horror experienced at home. It was hard to understand how this man, the man who taught me how to hit a golf ball and catch a baseball could turn into a monster after a few drinks. I hated the fact that my father loved alcohol more than he loved me. I had no understanding, after all the hurt and pain my father has caused, why I still loved him. Did I do something to deserve the abuse? If I made better grades in school or scored more points on the field, would he stop hurting me? I was only a child, but what could I do to make it all stop?

Children are hurt every day by people who should love them. It doesn't make sense to me now and it didn't make sense to me then. I do know and believe in my heart that I did not deserve the abuse I received at the hands of my father. I want you to know, that you do not deserve to be hurt either. Sometimes adults, even those we love, do things to hurt children. Is it fair? No! Do those children deserve that type of treatment? Absolutely NOT! But it happens . . . and it happens all too often.

Through the years when I think back at my childhood, I remember the happy times and sometimes I think about the bad. Just like you, those scars will always be there on the inside but that does not mean I can't move forward. It doesn't mean YOU can't move forward. Those memories do not have to consume me and my thoughts. You are not defined by those terrible moments from your childhood. Even though what happened was horrific, you can use it for good. You can allow yourself to be compassionate toward others. You can reach out to those who are in need and understand with a kind and loving heart what they are feeling. You can be and do anything you want. You can and already are someone's hero.

I know what some of you are feeling. You think you are damaged goods because somebody hurt you. You think you aren't worth it because someone said mean things and did horrible things to you and told you not to tell. Listen closely to what I am about to say: *don't let those other thoughts come sneaking in.* You are loved EXACTLY where you are at this very moment. You are appreciated for who you are right this very minute . . . not the person you might become, but the person you are right NOW. Yes, the scars are there and sometimes they hurt but what matters the most is knowing and understanding that you are loved and you are capable of great things.

Many times, when bad things happen to us or we are told bad things happened to someone else we keep quiet. Sometimes we just don't want to get involved, other times we are scared of what may happen if we tell. The children and adults who come to Stepping Stone and share their heartache have chosen to stand up for children. It may be a three-year-old little girl, a rough and tough teenage boy, or a scared mom who decides to share their experience. These people have chosen to tell because they want to prevent the terrifying horror from happening to others. It's not easy to open up and tell a complete stranger how someone has hurt you. Big brothers tell their teacher at school about their experience because they don't want to see it happen to their little brother. Big sisters speak up and tell their mom about stepdad coming into their room at night because they know their little sister might be the next victim. Whatever the reason and whatever the circumstance, children, teenagers, and adults chose to stand up and speak out for children. Because of you, those bad things that happened won't continue because YOU chose to tell. When you decided to walk through those doors of Stepping Stone, you immediately became a hero to me and many others.

Heroes come in all shapes and sizes. Some are big, some are small. Some are tough and some are sensitive. Some shout their experience with anger and frustration. Some quietly whisper because they are scared and ashamed. It doesn't matter how you speak up. It doesn't matter why you tell. However, it matters that you chose to share your experience. It matters that you chose to stop the abuse.

You are far more brave and courageous than any of those stars or celebrities that we saw in Hollywood. By taking that first step of telling your experience concerning abuse, you are helping to save the lives of other children. You are putting a stop to the terrible pain and sorrow you experienced. You are fearless and incredibly strong. By letting what happened to you be a source of healing instead of pain, you are standing up for that child whose voice cannot be heard because they are too scared or too ashamed to tell someone. Thank you for letting others hear your voice. Thank you for not letting yourself believe child abuse is someone else's problem. YOU are MY hero and I am glad you decided to tell your story.

We live in a world in which we need to share responsibility. It's easy to say, "It's not my child, not my community, not my world, not my problem." Then there are those who see the need and respond. I consider those people my heroes.
Mister Rogers (Fred Rogers)

Brooke Woods is the executive director of Stepping Stone Children's Advocacy Center in Dublin, Georgia.

CHAPTER 4

Butterflies, Hummingbirds, and Lots of Laughter

We "think we know" . . . we "think we know" . . . we "think we know" . . . Like the story about the little train trying to climb up the hill . . . "I think I can . . ." "I think I can . . ." I think I can . . ." We "think we know" how to help make your future journey in life better, healthier, stronger and happier, regardless of your past. What I know is that we all are doing our best to do the "right" thing at the "right" time for you and your family. Only you can let us know if we are getting it right and making a difference.

We all have a past we can't change. Love it or hate it, it's the truth. Whether you are a child, adolescent, adult, or senior, the one thing we all have in common beyond being human is that we all have a past full of experiences. Adults may be better at expressing past experiences than children, but it doesn't take away that even the youngest of us all, infants, have pasts which log every experience they have had.

The past exists but doesn't have to be in the present unless we bring it with us every day and drag it into our future. Some of our past experiences are so wonderful we will choose to bring them into our future and keep them close to us

> *"What has happened to each of us is done and can't be changed, but in the same sense we all have a future and that is what counts because each of us can choose what we do from this moment forward. Every moment of every day is yours to create and choose what will make you who you are and what you will be and do."*

every day as they propel us to feel better, do better, and want better. Other experiences from our past are so hurtful that we may not want to bring them into our future, but it can be difficult as they are so embedded into what our bodies, hearts, and souls have experienced.

As you read this you may be remembering the good, the bad, or even the ugly of what you have experienced in life so far. All of us, both young and old, are made up of everything we have experienced plus the dreams we have for the future. Past sorrow and pain can sometimes prevent us from realizing how strong we are in being able to truly make a difference in our futures.

What has happened to each of us is done and can't be changed, but in the same sense we all have a future and that is what counts because each of us can choose what we do from this moment forward. Every moment of every day is yours to create and choose what will make you who you are and what you will be and do.

You are not your past nor does your past define who you are. It is a part of what you have experienced but not what you have to carry into your future, which is an open book and a journey you can create and build with anything you wish.

There's a song I use to sing when I was a child and it went like this:

When I was just a little girl, I asked my mother what would I be?
Would I be pretty? Would I be rich? And here's what she said to me
Que sera sera, whatever will be will be, the future's not ours to see,
Que sera sera; what will be will be.

Your future *to be* is unlimited. It is as unique as you are, and will be your own journey and in part, for all of us, is a journey of healing. For your future I wish for you three things: *the hope of a butterfly, the strength of a hummingbird, and the healing of laughter.*

My first wish for you is that you will always *keep the butterfly effect of hope* close to your heart forever. Butterflies are so unique, just like you. A butterfly starts life as a very small egg. Some are round, some are oval, but each is different and unique depending upon what type of butterfly it is. You are as unique as a butterfly and will have changes in your life too.

After a butterfly egg hatches, it becomes a caterpillar. Caterpillars spend their days growing strong and working toward entering the next stage of their life. As you are growing you are also learning and exploring the world around you so you can grow strong too. It's funny because as adults we think only children are growing and changing; however, as grownups we also continue to grow and change throughout our life.

Once the caterpillar is strong enough, it enters into a phase that is the coolest of all, known as the pupa stage or the cocoon stage. Inside the cocoon, the caterpillar is protected and safe, undergoing wonderful changes and transforming to become a beautiful butterfly with wings. When the caterpillar has completely changed into a butterfly, it sheds its cocoon. The newly-formed butterfly will give its wings time to rest and strengthen so it can start working and flapping as it takes flight and soar. You also will grow strong, fly, and soar one day.

There will be times when you will want to create your very own cocoon like a butterfly and protect yourself from the world and what you have experienced.

This is true for both children and grownups; we all need to feel safe and protected regardless of how old we are. You may fear what might happen through a memory you have, a dream you experience, a passing thought, or even something someone says in passing. Like a butterfly, you need to know it is okay to retreat and stay in your cocoon at times. Feeling safe and protected is good and helps us all grow stronger. Butterflies are great at protecting themselves by realizing the time when their cocoon is their best friend and the safest place to be, and you will know this too.

Remember that like a butterfly you will, one day, shed your cocoon and fly. You will feel strong and the wings you grow will allow you to move forward and shed the fear that may have kept you in your cocoon. So if you ask, how do you become a butterfly? The answer is one day you will want to fly so much that you will be willing to give up being a caterpillar and take flight. You will feel so tired of being stuck in the same situation, the same sadness or hurtful place that you will realize shedding your past experiences and allowing yourself to heal will allow you to soar.

My second wish for you is that you always remember the *strength in your voice*, and your voice matters above all else in your healing. So many people, usually trying to be helpful, will share what they think you should say, what you should do, or how you should feel. Sometimes the voices from others may be so loud that you can't hear your own and will forget that the *most important* voice is yours!

Your voice is what you will hear the most and the loudest and it will direct you in your future journey that is yours to create. Your voice may be thoughts in your head, words that you write or words you speak out loud. No matter what form your voice is in it is yours and the most important of all voices you will ever listen to.

The hummingbird is one of the smallest birds in the world, and yet it can flap its wings over fifty times a second and create a humming sound that is called the voice of the hummingbird. We are all in awe of the beauty of a hummingbird as it is so small and can stay in one spot and fly like it is in suspension. The reality is the hummingbird's voice is loud and strong as each flap of the wing is purposeful and propels it forward in life. It takes huge amounts of energy for the hummingbird to flap its wings to move as its voice is created through the beautiful humming sound the flapping creates.

Like a hummingbird, as a child you are small or as an adult with a wounded past or painful present, you may feel small and weak; so it may take all your energy and courage to make your voice loud enough to be heard. You may need to be reminded that you can and need to make your voice be heard. You may talk, shout, or even have to scream to be heard, but *your voice is the most important voice you will* share with others, and most importantly, *listen to* as you live through your past, stand tall in the present, and travel your future journey full of promise.

My final wish for you is the *healing impact of laughter*. Have you ever laughed so hard you cried? Have you ever cried so hard you started laughing? Life has a way of making us cry when we don't want to and laugh at times when we shouldn't, but in the end both crying and laughing are good for your soul, your heart, and your well-being. I wish for you a hand to hold and safe place to cry when you need to. But more importantly *I wish for your laughter*. Even in the midst of sorrow and loss, laughter can be so healing. Search for the laughter in life, the absurd or craziness that makes no sense but does no harm and allows for laughter. Every moment of laughter will allow you to heal from the inside out. You deserve to be happy and laugh!

We "think we know" . . . we "think we know". . . we "think we know". . . and we do all we can to try and do the right thing at the right time to make a difference for children and their families. Sometimes we get it right and sometimes we need to try harder, but we always are doing our best and here to help. Only you can let us know if we are making it better for you and your family.

There's a great nursery rhyme that goes:

Humpty Dumpty sat on the wall
Humpty Dumpty had a great fall
All the king's horses and all the king's men
Couldn't put Humpty together again

I like to think that Humpty Dumpty didn't need all the king's horses and all the king's men anymore, after they all tried and helped as much as they could to put him/her back together again. Humpty Dumpty, like you, took the help he/she received and used their newfound strength and voice to soar into a future full of hope, healing, and laugher but knowing all along that we are always here to help whenever we are needed.

Jinger Robins is the executive director of SafePath Children's Advocacy Center in Marietta, Georgia.

CHAPTER 5

Forget About Forgetting

Each of us has defining moments in our lives; times when afterward our world is never the same. Some are good and some aren't so good. Think about this: What is the best thing that ever happened to you? What is the worst? These things we easily remember, but the everyday, run-of-the-mill events don't typically register with us.

For example (depending on your age), do you remember where you were and what you were doing when 9/11/2001 happened? What about when the Challenger exploded? When John F. Kennedy, Robert Kennedy, or Dr. Martin Luther King Jr. was assassinated? You probably weren't actually present for any of these events but when you think about them, your guts may become a knot; the fear and uncertainty are remembered. Life as we knew it had changed. Our innocence and invincibility were gone. While we don't dwell on these unimaginable event(s), we often remember them clearly.

This applies to abuse situations as well. Children and youth often feel fear, shame, and confusion or possibly physical pain. Parents feel guilty for not realizing what was happening to their children or for what acts were committed. Just as someone's death eventually gets

> "*Ignoring trauma is like dealing with your "junk drawer" at home. If the painful thoughts come to mind and you try to shove them down back into the drawer, eventually the drawer gets way too full. The drawer gets messy. It gets to the point where you would rather just not open the drawer.*"

easier to talk about or remember, talking about and remembering abusive incidents get easier to handle. Many times we can look at the lessons we learned from the experience at some point afterward.

Abuse and the resulting trauma are painful subjects. Abuse and trauma are like a splinter in your finger—you have to dig around to get the splinter out and IT HURTS! If you leave the splinter in your skin, infection may set in and parts of your body may become poisoned. Maybe your entire body will be affected so that major medical treatment is needed. But once the splinter is removed, using the right tools in the right setting, the spot begins to heal. A scar may be left, the area may be sore for a while, but the healing process does start and you may have to take care of the wound for a bit.

Ignoring trauma is like dealing with your "junk drawer" at home. If the painful thoughts come to mind and you try to shove them down back into the drawer, eventually the drawer gets way too full. The drawer gets messy. It gets to the point where you would rather just not open the drawer. It is difficult to keep everything packed down when you try to close the drawer after stuffing one more thing in it. Things may get turned sideways or stick up too high and it becomes a problem to even open the drawer. At times, you may even forget everything that is stuffed in that drawer. If you do remember a particular thing is in the drawer, you may not want to open the drawer because all of the other "junk" you will have to go through to find whatever it is you want or need. You often decide it is not worth the effort at that particular time to deal with the things in the drawer. You definitely know that you need to clean out the drawer, but you really do NOT want to do that. It seems to be more of a job than you can handle. Then one day, you open the drawer and everything inside explodes out. So many things fly out—some that you see, some that you cannot see, some land close by, some are scattered all over the room. It is a mess to sort through, and it usually happens at the most inopportune time. You wonder why you didn't do something sooner, when it would have been easier to handle and there was less "junk" to clean up and go through. It would not have taken so much time and effort. Now you must sort through everything that was in the drawer and decide what you want to do with it. You may relive the experiences tied to the "junk" as you decide what to do with each piece and feelings may be strong at times. You can no longer deny that these feelings were not important at the time you shoved them into the drawer and are still powerful.

With trauma, not talking about the event often creates more embarrassment and shame. Children think that if something is not talked about, it must really be horrible or bad because we do talk about some other things that are "bad," but not this topic. Parents often do not know what to do or say for fear they could make the situation worse or feel inadequate and/or guilty. But saying I love you, I wish this hadn't happened, it's not your fault, I believe you, we will work this out together, or I wish I had seen the signs that something was wrong will help a child or teen start to heal.

If only part of the family deals with the trauma, it will be like trying to put together a jigsaw puzzle with missing pieces. The child victim cannot be the only one in therapy because there are other family members who have conflicting and confusing thoughts about what occurred. The parents often feel guilty or angry, have the need to "make things right again" or "go away", and may do things that are not beneficial for anyone in the long run. The spousal relationship may also suffer, especially if it is a relative who was the perpetrator. Too often, the parent who is related to the perpetrator gets blamed for allowing the child to be around the perpetrator or feels guilty for allowing access. That parent's relatives may be angry at the parent and want the parent to support the perpetrator but not the victim. They may be angry that family secrets have been revealed or the family was not allowed to handle a "family matter." Siblings may be jealous of the attention the traumatized brother or sister gets or they may be angry if there are lifestyle changes involved. Some siblings feel guilty or responsible for the abuse of another sibling if they didn't tell about the things that they saw or heard but didn't fully understand. All the family needs to be involved in the healing process at some point, whether individually or as a family unit.

All family members feel betrayed when abuse occurs because it is very likely that the accused is a friend or relative that was trusted. We don't leave our kids with people we don't know or don't trust, so who would even think that abuse would happen? If the accused had been abused in the past or had made others feel uncomfortable, you still don't think this person would do something to *your* child. This is the betrayal. Losing the relationship may be the most difficult part of the healing and understanding for all of the family. It is often as if the perpetrator has to be "dead" to the victim and his or her family as there can be no contact. Children may not be able to interact with cousins, close friends, and other relatives. If the perpetrator was very involved with the family, the good things about the person will be remembered and missed and may even seem to outweigh the "bad" things that happened. The close relationship of the perpetrator to the victim and family will often be missed on some level. Also impacting the victim and his or her family are holiday gatherings and family reunions. Other family members may not understand why all cannot forgive and forget. The extended family is also deeply affected by the disclosure, resulting safety plans and possible arrest of the perpetrator. Anger and hard feelings may not be openly expressed but are often felt by the victim and his/her parents. Too often the victim feels guilty for disclosing and causing such chaos and broken relationships.

Many times when a child is abused, the parent who was molested as a child will experience the same feelings they had when it happened to them. The powerlessness, fear, and anger resurface. When this happens the parent also needs help getting through their own trauma to help the child.

It is very likely that your child will need "tune-ups" as his or her life progresses. Often times at puberty, the start of dating, the time of engagement and/or marriage, intimacy and childbirth, there is the need for more therapy as each of these steps brings its own factors into play, such as trust, sexual feelings, etc.

While individual and family counseling are the best resources and are often offered at no cost to the family, there are other resources to use along with counseling. For example, there are online resources available 24/7, as well as other support groups in many communities.

Parents must be aware that teen victims, both male and female, may self-harm to try to release inner pain. Some youth become anorexic, trying to gain a feeling of control. Others may have explosive anger and outbursts— beyond that which is typical. Others withdraw and keep to themselves.

Some may begin to use alcohol and/or drugs to numb the inner pain. Some may feel they have no control over their bodies and become sexually active without considering the consequences. Each child and teen is different, so a parent must be able to recognize the changes in behaviors in his/her child.

Parents need to hold the boundaries that have always been in place and keep the rules and lines intact. Since the child's or youth's boundaries have been broken, as have the parents to a certain extent, the young person needs to know that boundaries are still in place. Don't feel it is okay to let the rules slide because of what has happened—show you care enough to provide safety, protection, and rules. This will let the young person know that they have value in your eyes.

Kids, if your parent chooses the accused over you, you have another betrayal and loss to work through. As hard as it will be, you will eventually have to understand and accept your parent's selfishness and possible past abuse, but you don't have to like it. One day, your parent will realize what he/she has lost. You cannot change anyone, only your response to people and their acts. Let your parent go when it is best for you, and build new relationships with those who care for and will protect you. Look at the other life choices your parent has made—were they always the best decision for all or is it a pattern for him/her?

Mourn your losses because that is what abuse creates—all kinds of losses. Dr. Elisabeth Kubler-Ross said in *On Death and Dying* (1974) the stages of grief are: denial, anger, bargaining, depression, and acceptance. You will move back and forth among the stages as you heal. You don't move from one to the next then the next. One day you may find yourself in acceptance and anger then depression the next. THIS IS NORMAL. Keep seeking help.

When your life is not consumed by what happened, you are moving on but you don't forget what happened. Do not be ashamed of what happened—it wasn't your fault. The lies, trickery, and manipulation were beyond your ability to recognize and understand. Your parents probably did not see or recognize what was happening either and they are older and (hopefully) wiser than you.

Use your experience to help others—there is nothing better than to have a friend or ally who has been through the same thing. You can be part of a support group in your community, church, or synagogue, or start one with your friend and ally. You'll be amazed at the strength that you really do have. Volunteer at a child advocacy center or with CASA (Court Appointed Special Advocates) and be an ear for others, a voice for those who cannot speak for themselves, and a shoulder for support or tears.

You will probably never forget what happened to you, but with counseling, time, and supportive people around you, you will learn to live with the memory but without all the guilt, fear, shame, and embarrassment. This is when you have the power and the perpetrator no longer does. If you try to forget about the abuse and try to go through it alone, the perpetrator maintains the power in many ways and controls your life and your choices for years to come.

Be ready to become strong even if you don't feel anywhere close to strong right now. Don't try to forget about what happened—you can't. Accept the available support until you feel strong enough to work through and live with what happened on your own. It takes a long time for some people, and the longer you hold on to the negative, the longer it may take in therapy. Once you are stronger and can think and talk about what happened without becoming totally unglued, it will be your turn to help others. Just remember how you once felt since you never truly forget. You've learned to cope and live stronger than many.

Remember that!

Julia Houston is the executive director of the Pataula Center for Children in Blakely, Georgia.

CHAPTER 6

It Takes Courage

Every one of us is unique in our own special way, just as *every child is different*! Every child has the potential to react differently and every child has the potential to behave differently. I know I certainly react differently than any one of my five sisters to any type of situation!

With that said, there have been a number of children who come into our Child Advocacy Center (CAC) feeling as if they are the only one in the entire world who has ever had something painful, scary, or sad happen to them, and everyone they come in contact with just "knows" what has happened by looking at them—like it's a neon sign on their forehead announcing to the world exactly what it was that happened to them. Sometimes it's just the opposite, and they feel certain no one will believe the event they are about to explain to the forensic interviewer. When a child walks into a CAC, they often walk into the unknown. They often know why they are there, but they aren't quite sure what to expect once they actually walk through that door.

It takes courage to stand up and speak; but it also takes courage to sit down and listen. What a profound statement written by Sir Winston Churchill. It takes courage for a child to tell someone when they

> "*Show your child you support them, and really support them. The painful, scary, or sad event does not define them, and do not let it define you either. One of the greatest indicators of the healing process is that you, the caregiver, believe and support the child.*"

have been hurt, mistreated, or violated. It also takes courage for the non-offending caregivers to sit down, listen, and hear what the child is saying. It takes tremendous courage to listen to your child when they are telling you about something bad, scary, or painful, or that someone they loved and trusted violated that love and trust, or that someone you loved and trusted violated that love and trust. You both need to listen to each other.

Often you feel guilt and shame. "Why didn't I know?" "Why didn't my child tell me sooner?" "How did I allow this to happen?"

Don't blame yourself, and most importantly, don't blame your child. Individuals who hurt children often threaten the child or someone they love (you) with physical harm or tell the child that no one will believe them or that the child is responsible or if the child "tells," the perpetrator will go to jail. Think about how hard it was for you, the non-offending caregiver, to hear what the child has said. Just imagine how hard it was for the child to tell you. Now that your child has told you about the abuse or neglect, the most important thing you can do is to believe what your child is telling you and get them to the appropriate professionals as soon as possible.

There are forty-six wonderful CACs all across the state of Georgia. These centers are designed to be safe, neutral, child-friendly centers where the children can tell their story. Child Advocacy Centers are staffed with trained professionals who care about your child and want your child to feel safe and comfortable telling their story while not making them tell the story multiple times. Often what happens after the disclosure of abuse or neglect can be just as "traumatic" as the actual abuse or neglect. CACs are "trauma-informed" and work to minimize fear or uncertainty felt by the child or the non-offending caregiver. Often we are afraid of what we do not know. This can be a difficult time for you and your child, and you can make it less scary by preparing your child for what will happen at the CAC. As Eleanor Roosevelt said so eloquently, *"You gain strength, courage, and confidence by every experience in which you really stop to look fear in the face. You must do the thing which you think you cannot do."*

When you and your child arrive at the CAC, the staff will be expecting you. There will be paperwork to be completed, and the team is happy to answer any questions you may have. Waiting areas are child friendly and comfortable. Every effort is made to schedule interviews to ensure as much privacy as possible. Assure your child that they are safe and they can trust the child advocate, the forensic interviewer, and others on the CAC staff.

By definition, a child advocate is someone who supports a child. You and your child may be wondering if this child advocate is someone they can trust. The child advocate is working for the best interest of your child. Make sure you, as the child's caregiver, reassure your child that they can trust the child advocate. They may ask, "What is a forensic interview, and how do I know I can tell them my story and not feel judged?" You should assure them they will meet with a forensic interviewer who is a trained professional and who is neutral. Let your children know they can trust this team member and that it is okay with you if they tell their story; encourage your children to tell them the truth. All child advocacy centers throughout the state of Georgia are held to the same standards, so all child advocates and forensic interviewers are held to the same criteria and guidelines. It should be comforting to you as a caregiver to know that the Children's Advocacy Center of Georgia makes sure you are receiving the best services possible from every child advocacy center consistently throughout the state.

Once the paperwork is complete, the child will have a forensic interview. As defined by the Juvenile Justice Bulletin, a forensic interview is a developmentally-sensitive and legally-sound method of gathering factual information regarding allegations of abuse or exposure to violence. The interview is conducted by a competently trained, neutral professional utilizing research and practiced-informed techniques as part of a larger investigative process. At first glance this can seem like a lot of information to digest. However, what this means is that a professional who cares about your child will have a conversation with your child and allow them to tell their story. The forensic interviewer may ask open-ended questions while having a conversation driven by your child. The interviewer is trained and sensitive to avoid causing secondary trauma to your child. It's why CACs are much more preferable to a sterile law enforcement facility. While having the conversation, the interviewers are using their skills to help gather factual information to assist the multidisciplinary team in the investigation process. Interviewers are trained to not ask questions or make statements that may jeopardize the investigation. The forensic interview is a safe place to tell their story. There is no "blame" or "judgment." There are no "wrong answers" and the children can use any language with which they are comfortable. After the interview, continue to assure your child that he or she is safe, that you believe them, and that this is not their fault. If they want to discuss it, let them. If they don't, respect that. Because remember, this is yet another blasted door to the unknown they have had to walk through.

After the forensic interview, your child may be referred to a therapist. This does not mean that your child is damaged, broken, or won't have a productive, successful life. It's quite the opposite actually. Specialized therapies are effective in helping children "recover" from traumatic experiences. Just like you helped your child understand what happens at the CAC, help your child to understand that therapy is a "safe place" to talk about their feelings, confusions, or fears. It is not uncommon for children to blame themselves, be scared, or avoid places or people that remind them of the abuse or neglect. They may also act in ways that seem strange to adults. If you have a very young child, sometimes they "lose" skills they have mastered like pottying. At any age, it's not uncommon for them to become scared of the dark. Sometimes they "act out" the abuse. They may become more aggressive, or they may act as if nothing has changed. Again, every child is different. A trained therapist will help you understand what is going on with your child and help "normalize" the behaviors. A therapist can also help you deal with your feelings and fears as a caregiver associated with the abuse or neglect.

After you have left the CAC, the very best things you can do is believe what the child has said as being the truth and assure them that nobody else knows unless they choose to tell. There is no flashing neon sign telling anyone something has happened to them. Neither teachers nor classmates have to know unless they want them to know. They do not have to tell anyone unless they want to. At home, if they want to talk about it, then let them. If they do not want to talk about what happened, do not make them talk about it. Make certain they understand the fact they walk the same, they talk the same, and they are still the very same person they were before. However, they may feel different on the inside, and getting them to a specially trained therapist is an important step in the healing process, to help with healing the inside. You, the non-offending caregiver, need to assure the child that what has happened to them is NOT their fault. Make sure they understand they never "did anything" to make something happen and they never "did anything" to deserve it. Do not let your child feel responsible for the actions of the abuser. Do not let them take on that responsibility, just as you should not take on that responsibility.

Just as it is important that you make sure your child sees a therapist, it is important also you take care of yourself. The caregiver's need to see a therapist can be as important as it is for the child. The healing process is just that, a process. Some families believe that once the disclosure happens it should be over. In reality, the healing has just begun. Just as disclosure is a process, healing is also a process. Healing will not always happen in just one session. Only you and your therapist can decide what your treatment plan should be. It is just as important for you, the non-offending caregiver, to be able to heal and cope with the event as it is for your child. You have to be understanding of what your child is going through, but also be mindful of what *you* are experiencing. You have to take care of yourself in order to be effective in taking care of your child.

The event which brought you to the CAC may have been painful, scary, or sad to both you and your child, and what your child may be feeling is perfectly normal. They may be acting differently, and it may not make sense to you. But it is okay. It doesn't mean they won't ever be okay. Don't be hard on yourself. Give yourself a break every once in a while. Stay away from social media for a while. With your help and the help of a trained professional, it will be okay. And your child needs to know you really believe that. While everyone will react differently, we all just want to feel loved and valued. Show your child you support them, and *really* support them. The painful, scary, or sad event does not define them, and do not let it define you either. One of the greatest indicators of the healing process is that you, the caregiver, believe and support the child. Believe what the child has told you as being the truth. REALLY believe them. It is not just believing your child will get better, but really believing your child's story and acting on it. Again, respect your child's wishes of who they want to share their story with; it is theirs to share. You may feel alone at times, but please know your child advocacy center is only a phone call away, with referrals and resources to help point you back in the direction that is best for your family's healing process. Remember, as Taylor Swift said, "Just be yourself. There is no one better."

Lelee Phinney is the executive director of the Gateway Children's Advocacy Center in Cordele, Georgia.

CHAPTER 7

Personally

I recently found myself reflecting on my childhood; being a survivor of child physical, sexual, and emotional abuse is not a subject that is normally discussed or shared with many people.

At the age of forty-six and being a child advocate and forensic interviewer for the last ten years, I have realized that kids need to know that they cannot only survive but overcome their circumstances.

My father died before my second birthday. A lot of people said that my mom never really recovered from his death. My mom made A LOT of bad choices.

My earliest memory is looking into a keyhole and seeing my stepdad choking my mom. I was around three or four. I remember running about three blocks to where my grandparents lived. My grandparents were everything to me and my brother. I just remember my papa going down to the apartment to find out what was going on, but by the time he got there my stepdad was gone. This began the first of MANY times my mother would leave my stepdad

> *"Be an overcomer, forgive yourself. It's okay to be angry or sad, just don't get stuck there. If I could tell my younger self anything is that it's okay to feel, it's okay to be angry, to cry, to scream to yell. What's not okay is to deny yourself your feelings and to never heal from the hurt."*

for a few days and then go right back. This became very routine. At that time he did not abuse us; until he moved us away from our grandparents into a small, very rural town.

Then life changed: my stepdad began verbal and emotional abusing, then came the physical abuse. I never knew from one day to the next what to expect, he drank almost every day and just seemed so angry. Every night when he would get home we had to be sitting at the dining room table and no one ate until he did. Now this doesn't seem extreme except for the fact that most nights he would get home really late. And the weekends were the worst because we were lucky if he came home by midnight, and true to form he would be highly intoxicated. Those nights were so long and terrifying, he would come in, throw all the food on the floor, curse, and beat my mother. I was terrified, I would hide under the table or at least try. My brother was at the age that he would try to defend my mom; this usually ended badly, with black eyes and busted lips.

I remember during the summer we were not allowed in the house until dark; we would ride our bikes all over the place and sit in the fields across from the house and try to plot how we could run away. Mind you we were five and eight at the time. I loved my mama, but I could not understand WHY. Why would she allow him to hurt not only her but me? These times were very confusing; when she left him I was supposed to hate him, and then when she went back I was supposed to love him. It was our grandparents that always rescued us when my mom would leave. Then the worst thing happened, my papa died. What would we do now? Now we had NO ONE.

This is when things started getting worse for me. I would wake up in the middle of the night to him standing over my bed, holding my covers up just looking at me. I was six when that started. I didn't understand why he was doing this; I was terrified to say anything to him or to my mom. Then things got stranger: I was about seven now and he would want me to ride off with him, ALONE. He would become so intoxicated he would let me drive home. I learned how to drive a stick-shift truck. (Thank God it was a tiny little Datsun.) It was during these outings that he began rubbing my back and hug on me and he would tell me that my mama said she didn't love me; he would tell me that my mama was a whore and she was sorry. I didn't even know what a whore was, but it made me angry with my mom. Crazy, right? I didn't know then that he was conditioning me for what was coming. One night my mom was in the tub and he and I were watching television, when he wanted me to come lay on the couch with him. I didn't want to but knew if I refused I would get smacked; he grabbed me and started putting his hand down my pants and he touched my vagina. I fought feverishly to get away, and in the process he busted my lip. He told me I better keep my mouth shut. I went into the bathroom where my mom was but could not say anything; I felt a FEAR like I had never known before. My mom asked me what happened, I couldn't tell her, I just told her we were wrestling around and I accidentally busted my lip.

I was used to having to lie about bruises, black eyes, busted lips especially to the school. I was never allowed to go with anyone anywhere, not his family or ours. We could not go to church. He didn't want people to know he was hurting us, but people knew. I know they wanted to help but didn't know how or were too scared to get involved.

One night when I was about eight or nine, my stepdad had started beating my mom and somehow they ended up in my bedroom. This night would change me: I was sitting on my bed and my mother ran in trying to get away from him. As he came through the door, I saw the pistol. As me and mama sat there clutched as hard as possible, he raised the gun to our heads, he told us he could kill us and no one would know or care. He was probably right about the knowing part because by this time my mom was not allowed to talk to her family. We begged for our lives. That night something in me changed, I was not afraid anymore, I had taken all I could take. I told him to leave us alone or to shoot me, but I could no longer live this way.

I honestly don't know why he didn't kill me. That next day we left to go to my grandmother's house. But this would not be the end of it. After a few months my mom was actually thinking of going back. I know you're saying, are you kidding me? I knew I had to tell someone about him touching me, I could not go back. I finally became brave enough to tell someone. I am not sure how the Department of Family and Children Services came into the picture, but I remember sitting at a table with a case worker, my mom, and my grandmother. The case worker asked me about what had happened, I told her; my mom said I was liar. I was crying so hard I could barely catch my breath. The case worker gave my mom two options: get rid of him or lose us. This part I will never forget for as long as I live; my mom told them she would have to think about it. At that moment my heart was broken into a million pieces. Needless to say, that was the longest weekend ever. She divorced my stepdad, but she let me know constantly that she loved him and still thought I was a liar; I was nine. For the most part, my mom and I didn't really have any type of relationship after this. I spent most of my time going from house to house with different relatives.

Thank God for my little tiny eighty-pound grandmother. She was always my saving grace. I lived with her until she passed away, then I went from family member to friends, staying wherever I could. I don't think I ever really felt grounded.

Through all of this I could have allowed myself to make extremely poor choices as she did, but I decided very young that I would never allow anyone to treat me or my kids that way. I could tell you that everything was sunshine and rainbows from there, but the truth is I had a long way to go. There was a fear of trusting anyone, a fear of people finding out; I never spoke of my past with anyone. I always came off as this tough girl, and for the most part I guess I was because I had to fight myself daily: I was hurt, I was scared, I felt betrayed by the person who is supposed to love me the most. If I had given in to my emotions I would have crumbled, so instead I kept pushing them down, never really dealing with them. Don't get me wrong, I spent a good bit of my late teens and early twenties being angry, but then I realized this was just hurting me. At nineteen I decided I needed structure in my life, so I joined the United States Army. I loved the routine of things. You knew each day what was ahead of you, no huge surprises.

At twenty I got married and had my daughter when I was twenty-one, I had not had much contact with my mom during this time; however, when she found out I was pregnant she wanted to be in my life again. It was really hard to say yes. That was a changing point in my life; after having my daughter, my mother and I had a decent relationship. She had to work to earn my trust, but she was determined to and honestly she was like the mother I had wanted my whole life. She treated my daughter like a princess. She babysat a lot for me after I divorced and was a single mom.

The weird thing is we never talked about any of it; it's like that time in our lives never happened. Not once did my mom even acknowledge the things that happened to me. I guess it was denial, or the mere fact of it being too painful to relive.

Believe it or not I was able to eventually forgive my mom. In 2007 my mom was diagnosed with lung cancer. In 2008 she held my hand, and for the first time ever she apologized for not believing me and for allowing me to be hurt like that and she told me how sorry she was that she had not told me sooner. My mom died December 3, 2008.

I think about how I could have allowed this to literally consume me. But what I have learned is that you don't have to let your current circumstances define your future. Be an overcomer, forgive yourself. It's okay to be angry or sad, just don't get stuck there. If I could tell my younger self anything, it is that it's okay to feel, it's okay to be angry, to cry, to scream to yell. What's not okay is to deny yourself your feelings and to never heal from the hurt.

Sometimes the hardest thing to do is to look into a mirror and say, "I love you."

Carol Williford is the executive director of the Child Advocacy Center of Coffee County – Sadie's House, in Douglas, Georgia.

CHAPTER 8

Words of Wisdom to Help You on Your Journey to Healing: *100 Quotes to Inspire Those Recovering from Abuse*

During my early days as a therapist working with survivors of child sexual abuse, I had the opportunity to assist "Jane" (a pseudonym) on her journey to healing. "Jane" was a preteen when she disclosed sexual abuse at the hands of an adult uncle. The abuse had been going on for many years. In the midst of a heated argument with her parent about being disrespectful, Jane blurted out, "It's hard to pretend like you're in a good mood all the time when someone is always touching you." After Jane had the painful discussion with her parents about being molested, her parents reported the abuse to the police and an investigation ensued. Jane's abuser was arrested and charged with numerous crimes related to the abuse inflicted on Jane.

Jane felt relieved that her abuser would never touch her in that way again and that she would no longer have to carry the burden alone. All the while, Jane had a challenging road ahead of her as she continued to try and cope with the toll that the abuse had taken on her and how she felt about herself. Jane expressed intense feelings of grief, anger, self-doubt, regret, confusion, self-loathing, embarrassment, guilt, and, most of all, shame.

During our many months together in therapy, Jane fiercely and bravely worked to process through her trauma and to learn how to use new healthy coping skills to help her navigate her journey to healing. Despite making significant progress in therapy, Jane continued to report struggling with persistent, pervasive shame that would often flood her and overwhelm her when she least expected it. Jane needed assistance in establishing a new, kind, loving, compassionate, and forgiving relationship with herself. One of the ways that I assisted Jane in confronting and combating her shame was to assign daily homework. Jane's daily homework included reading quotes I had carefully selected that I thought could be helpful as she tried to replace her shame with a more positive and proud perception of her ability to survive, heal, and thrive. Perhaps a few of these quotes could be helpful to you as you travel along your own journey to healing.

Working through Shame

1. "We need never be ashamed of our tears."
   — Charles Dickens

2. "Don't judge yourself by what others did to you."
   — C. Kennedy, Omorphi

3. "If we can share our story with someone who responds with empathy and understanding, shame can't survive."
   — Brené Brown

4. "Shame is the lie someone told you about yourself."
   — Anais Nin

5. "We all make mistakes, have struggles, and even regret things in our past. But you are not your mistakes, you are not your struggles, and you are here NOW with the power to shape your day and your future."
   — Steve Maraboli

6. "Don't let yesterday take up too much of today."
   — John Wooden

7. "There are two kinds of guilt: the kind that drowns you until you're useless, and the kind that fires your soul to purpose."
   — Sabaa Tahir

8. "Perfectionism is a self-destructive and addictive belief system that fuels this primary thought: If I look perfect, and do everything perfectly, I

can avoid or minimize the painful feelings of shame, judgment, and blame."
— Brené Brown

9. "Of all the judgments we pass in life, none is more important than the judgment we pass on ourselves."
— Nathaniel Branden

10. "Instead of denying your shame and the feelings it engenders, bring it out into the light. Instead of feeling shame about your shame, work toward acceptance of it. Instead of constantly seeking approval and recognition from outside yourself, learn to value yourself from within."
—Beverly Engel

11. "It is not as much about who you used to be, as it is about who you choose to be."
—Sanhita Baruah

<u>Forgiving Yourself</u>

1. "Ultimately, the only person you must forgive is yourself. If you are still blaming yourself or feeling ashamed of the things you've done to cope, it's time to forgive yourself, to stop blaming the child that was vulnerable, the child who felt pleasure, the child who survived as best she could."
— Ellen Bass and Laura Davis

2. "True confession consists in telling our deed in such a way that our soul is changed in the telling it."
-Maude Perre

3. "When you slip up and let yourself back into old, toxic patterns of thinking, forgive yourself before you try to fix yourself."
— Vironika Tugaleva

4. "Be courageous enough to forgive yourself; never forget to be compassionate to yourself."
— Debasish Mridha

5. "It's time to forgive yourself for anything you're still feeling guilty about, anything you're still holding yourself responsible for. It wasn't your fault that you couldn't protect yourself. It wasn't your fault that you needed attention and affection."
    — Ellen Bass and Laura Davis

6. "I don't know if I continue, even today, always liking myself. But what I learned to do many years ago was to forgive myself. It is very important for every human being to forgive herself or himself because if you live, you will make mistakes - it is inevitable. But once you do and you see the mistake, then you forgive yourself and say, 'Well, if I'd known better I'd have done better,' that's all. So you say to people who you think you may have injured, 'I'm sorry,' and then you say to yourself, 'I'm sorry.' If we all hold on to the mistake, we can't see our own glory in the mirror because we have the mistake between our faces and the mirror; we can't see what we're capable of being. You can ask forgiveness of others, but in the end the real forgiveness is in one's own self.
    — Maya Angelou

7. "Letting go may sound so simple, but rarely is it a one-time thing. Just keep letting go, until one day it's gone for good."
    — Eleanor Brownn

8. "It's OK if you mess up. You should give yourself a break."
    — Billy Joel

9. "Bring it up, make amends, forgive yourself. It sounds simple, but don't think for a second that it is easy. Getting free from the tyranny of past mistakes can be hard work, but definitely worth the effort. And the payoff is health, wholeness and inner peace. In other words, you get your life back."
    — Steve Goodier

10. "Forgiveness is a gift to the one who is hurting."
    —Josee D'Amore

11. "Lack of forgiveness causes almost all of our self-sabotaging behaviors."
    —Mark Victor Hansen

12. "Be gentle with yourself, learn to love yourself, to forgive yourself, for only as we have the right attitude toward ourselves can we have the right attitude toward others."
    —Wilifred Peterson

13. "Forgiveness is giving up the hope that the past could have been any different, it's accepting the past for what it was, and using this moment and this time to help yourself move forward."
    —Oprah Winfrey

14. "Forgiveness is a gift you give yourself."
    —Tony Robbins

15. "Forgiveness does not change the past, but it does enlarge the future."
    —Deepak Chopra

16. "Forgiveness is not something you do for someone else, it's something you do for yourself."
    —Jim Beaver

Having Love, Acceptance, and Compassion for Yourself

1. "You yourself, as much as anybody in the entire universe, deserve your love and affection."
   —Buddha

2. "Love yourself first and everything else falls into line. You really have to love yourself to get anything done in this world."
   —Lucille Ball

3. "If only you could sense how important you are to the lives of those you meet; how important you can be to people you may never even dream of. There is something of yourself that you leave at every meeting with another person."
   —Fred Rogers

4. "What lies behind us and what lies before us are tiny matters compared to what lies within us."
   —Ralph Waldo Emerson

5. "Why should we worry about what others think of us, do we have more confidence in their opinions than we do our own?"
   —Brigham Young

6. "To establish true self-esteem we must concentrate on our successes and forget about the failures and the negatives in our lives."
   —Denis Waitley

7. "Our self-respect tracks our choices. Every time we act in harmony with our authentic self and our heart, we earn our respect. It is that simple. Every choice matters."
   —Dan Coppersmith

8. "Don't rely on someone else for your happiness and self-worth. Only you can be responsible for that. If you can't love and respect yourself – no one else will be able to make that happen. Accept who you are – completely; the good and the bad – and make changes as YOU see fit – not because you think someone else wants you to be different."
   —Stacey Charter

9. "Never bend your head. Always hold it high. Look the world straight in the face."
   —Helen Keller

10. "You have been criticizing yourself for years, and it hasn't worked. Try approving of yourself and see what happens."
    —Louise L. Hay

11. "To love oneself is the beginning of a life-long romance."
    —Oscar Wilde

12. "Be faithful to that which exists within yourself."
    —André Gide

13. "The most beautiful people we have known are those who have known defeat, known suffering, known struggle, known loss, and have found their way out of the depths. These persons have an appreciation, a sensitivity and an understanding of life that fills them with compassion, gentleness, and a deep loving concern. Beautiful people do not just happen."
—Elizabeth Kubler-Ross

14. "You're always with yourself, so you might as well enjoy the company."
—Diane Von Furstenberg

15. "No one can make you feel inferior without your consent."
—Eleanor Roosevelt

16. "You are very powerful, provided you know how powerful you are."
—Yogi Bhajan

17. "Trust yourself. You know more than you think you do."
—Benjamin Spock

18. "Your problem is you're . . . too busy holding onto your unworthiness."
—Ram Dass

19. "There came a time when the risk to remain tight in the bud was more painful than the risk it took to blossom."
—Anaïs Nin

20. "It took me a long time not to judge myself through someone else's eyes."
—Sally Field

21. "It is never too late to be what you might have been."
—George Eliot

22. "If you do not respect your own wishes, no one else will. You will simply attract people who disrespect you as much as you do."
—Vironika Tugaleva

23. "A moment of self-compassion can change your entire day. A string of such moments can change the course of your life."
—Christopher K. Germer

24. "The definition of success in life has many different meanings. Don't compare your journey to the journey of others. Only you know where the journey began and how very far you have come."
—Eleanor Brownn

25. "Self-compassion is simply giving the same kindness to ourselves that we would give to others."
—Christopher Germer

26. "Wanting to be someone else is a waste of the person you are."
—Marilyn Monroe

27. "What self-acceptance does is open up more possibilities of succeeding because you aren't fighting yourself along the way."
—Shannon Ables

28. "Self-acceptance means living the life you choose to live without worrying what others think about you. It doesn't matter what someone else thinks about you. What matters is what you think about yourself."
—Sadiqua Hamdan

29. "You can't build joy on a feeling of self-loathing."
—Ram Dass

30. "With self-acceptance, we have the ability to choose compassion and forgiveness over anger and self-hatred."
—Michelle Cruz-Rosado

31. "Did your mom ever tell you, 'If you can't say something nice, don't say anything'? She was right – and talking nicely also applies when you're talking to yourself, even inside your head."
—Victoria Moran

32. "No other love no matter how genuine it is, can fulfill one's heart better than unconditional self-love."
   —Edmond Mbiaka

33. "We all have the tendency to believe self-doubt and self-criticism, but listening to this voice never gets us closer to our goals. Instead, try on the point of view of a mentor or good friend who believes in you, wants the best for you, and will encourage you when you feel discouraged."
   —Kelly McGonigal

34. "As you become your own advocate and your own steward, your life will beautifully transform."
   —Miranda J. Barrett

35. "This revolutionary act of treating ourselves tenderly can begin to undo the aversive messages of a lifetime."
   —Tara Brach

36. "Today and onwards, I stand proud, for the bridges I've climbed, for the battles I've won, and for the examples I've set, but most importantly, for the person I have become. I like who I am now, finally, at peace with me. . ."
   —Heather James

37. "Who can truly respect those things that are no longer a part of you because of all your work to release them? Who can see the strength left behind in the wake of your unique struggles and obstacles? Who will see you for who you are, appreciating everything that is there, everything that is not, everything that can be, if you do not? Who else can?"
   —Vironika Tugaleva

38. "Do you want to meet the love of your life? Look in the mirror."
   —Byron Katie

39. "The privilege of a lifetime is being who you are."
   —Joseph Campbell

40. "The only person who can pull me down is myself, and I'm not going to let myself pull me down anymore."
    —C. JoyBell C.

41. "To be beautiful means to be yourself. You don't need to be accepted by others. You need to accept yourself."
    —Thich Nhat Hanh

42. "Believing in our hearts that who we are is enough is the key to a more satisfying and balanced life."
    —Ellen Sue Stern

43. "Friendship with oneself is all important, because without it one cannot be friends with anyone else in the world."
    —Eleanor Roosevelt

44. "You have brains in your head.
    You have feet in your shoes.
    You can steer yourself in any direction you choose.
    You're on your own.
    And you know what you know.
    You are the guy who'll decide where to go."
    —Dr. Seuss

45. "I now see how owning our story and loving ourselves through that process is the bravest thing that we will ever do."
    —Brené Brown

46. "You are beautiful. Know this. Anyone who tells you otherwise is simply lying. You are beautiful."
    —Steve Maraboli

47. "The kinder and more compassionate we are with ourselves, the more we can develop the courage to tolerate difficult things."
    —Beverly Engel

48. "Always remember you are braver than you believe, stronger than you seem, and smarter than you think."
—Christopher Robin

49. "You can't be brave if you've only had wonderful things happen to you."
—Mary Tyler Moore

50. "And once the storm is over, you won't remember how you made it through, how you managed to survive. You won't even be sure, whether the storm is really over. But one thing is certain. When you come out of the storm, you won't be the same person who walked in. That's what this storm's all about."
— Haruki Murakami

51. "You may encounter many defeats, but you must not be defeated. In fact, it may be necessary to encounter the defeats, so you can know who you are, what you can rise from, how you can still come out of it."
— Maya Angelou

52. "Someone once asked me how I hold my head up so high after all I've been through. I said, it's because no matter what, I am a survivor. Not a victim."
— Patricia Buckley

53. "If you celebrate your differentness, the world will, too. It believes exactly what you tell it—through the words you use to describe yourself, the actions you take to care for yourself, and the choices you make to express yourself. Tell the world you are one-of-a-kind creation who came here to experience wonder and spread joy. Expect to be accommodated."
—Victoria Moran

Taking Care of Yourself

1. "When you recover or discover something that nourishes your soul and brings joy, care enough about yourself to make room for it in your life."
—Jean Shinoda Bolen

2. "Self-care is never a selfish act—it is simply good stewardship of the only gift I have, the gift I was put on earth to offer to others."
—Parker Palmer

3. "A healthy self-love means we have no compulsion to justify to ourselves or others why we take vacations, why we sleep late, why we buy new shoes, why we spoil ourselves from time to time. We feel comfortable doing things which add quality and beauty to life."
—Andrew Matthews

4. "Don't ask yourself what the world needs, ask yourself what makes you come alive. And then go and do that. Because what the world needs is people who have come alive."
—Howard Washington Thurman

5. "There are days I drop words of comfort on myself like falling leaves and remember that it is enough to be taken care of by myself."
—Brian Andreas

6. "Taking good care of yourself means the people in your life receive the best of you rather than what is left of you."
—Lucille Zimmerman

7. "Nourishing yourself in a way that helps you blossom in the direction you want to go is attainable, and you are worth the effort."
—Deborah Day

8. "Sometimes being happy takes effort. Invest time and energy in yourself and your happiness."
—Amy Leigh Mercree

9. "We need to start treating ourselves how we deserve to be treated, even if you feel that no one else does. Prove to the world you are worth something by treating yourself with the utmost respect and hope that other people will follow your example. And even if they don't, at least one person in the world is treating you well: You."
—Carrie Hope Fletcher

10. "By honoring and responding to your natural and essential requirements for sleep, food, water and movement, you will rise out of the realm of survival into the world of fulfillment."
    —Miranda J. Barrett

11. "Anytime we can listen to true self and give the care it requires, we do it not only for ourselves, but for the many others whose lives we touch."
    — Parker J. Palmer

12. "Each positive thought, every vibrant attitude, all purposeful activities water the seeds for success along your path. You will encounter many seeds for success today. Pay attention to these and feed them appropriately. Then maintain their beautiful growth through conscious self-care."
    —Rebecca Gordon

13. "People often ask 'how is life treating you?' Perhaps the more accurate question is 'how are you treating yourself?'"
    —Sepi Tajima

14. "Stop what you are doing. Go outside and breathe. The world will not end if you take ten minutes for yourself."
    —Fawn Germer

15. "Taking care of yourself isn't about trying to become perfect. It's about realizing and honouring, in every moment, that you already are."
    —Vironika Tugaleva

16. "The greatest weapon against stress is our ability to choose one thought over another."
    —William James

17. "It's not selfish to love yourself, take care of yourself, and to make your happiness a priority. It's necessary."
    —Mandy Hale

18. "Invent your world. Surround yourself with people, color, sounds, and work that nourish you."
   —Susan Ariel Rainbow Kennedy

19. "Every day brings a chance for you to draw in a breath, kick off your shoes, and dance."
   —Oprah Winfrey

20. "Taking time to do nothing often brings everything into perspective."
   —Doe Zantamata

Amy Economopoulos is the executive director of the Anna Crawford Children's Center in Woodstock, Georgia.

CHAPTER 9

Finding Hope in the Failures

I think we failed you. The word failure is hard to say or admit but one seemingly needed to move on. Those of us in this profession are warriors. We want to fix pain, help those children who are hurt, and put away the bad guys or girls. We are experts in the field of children and development, families and abuse. Collectively, we do have immense knowledge, and yet there are times we get in our own way. Sometimes the knowledge we have accumulated gets in the way of seeing the real picture. Sometimes we can't see the real story through our glasses of expertise.

Yours was one of those stories. We heard you but didn't understand. You were an unwilling participant in all the events that brought you to us. Quietly you moved through the parts that were forced on you. Dark and gloomy, you refused to talk, refused to heal. Many times you changed your story. Through it all we stuck with our knowledge, our way of handling things. You were not something to be handled but we didn't know that until later.

Could we have changed anything to make a difference? The answer is obviously yes. We wonder, even now, was there another way? We know there were other ways, why couldn't we have seen it then?

"Your soul is beautiful. You were hurt but not broken. You have a life to lead that can go in many directions. You can choose to allow all this to define you, or you can choose to define yourself. Choose hope and living and next."

When you came to us, your beautiful soul was broken. Scarred inside, even your eyes were blank and hidden. You were like a rock in the middle of a raging sea. You were sad and empty but determined to stand against those that raged against you and yours. You wouldn't let anyone get close to you, even those that wanted to help. We wanted to help. Our time together was stormy, full of angst and chaos. While you were in our system, you showed us glimpses of something else, a smiling child and a happy family. You didn't give away much, only what you wanted to or perhaps thought you should. We tried everything we knew but we didn't change anything, did we? Was there anything we could have done to create a different outcome? Looking back, it seems the entire time you were visiting us you were in pain, confused, and angry. You left us the same way you came, with quiet dignity and stubborn resolve.

In our defense, we thought we knew best. We see children all the time. We are the experts. We know what's best, right? The system cannot be completely wrong, can it? See, we had this strategy. We thought that if you had just followed our plan you would be fine, at least that is what we told ourselves. We wanted to make sure you were safe, taken care of by the *right* people.

You had a plan that was different than what we had imagined. Yours was a story that was untold or deeper than what we were able to hear or decipher. We were wrong, the process was wrong for you. We see this as a huge failure. We thought we knew best. That was our biggest mistake. We didn't know best and we didn't have the perfect strategy. For you see, our perfect strategy fell apart. It wasn't perfect after all.

We had heard your story long before we saw your face. We painted a picture of what we thought your story would be and we gave it a name. It was your name. It was our picture. Of course you were going to have a sad face. You would be angry, or distant, or suicidal. Because we are subject experts, we already knew how you would act, talk, and think. Our picture, remember? Then you came through the doors. You were all that we had imagined and so much more. We all fell in love with you. You were a beautiful, sad, dark, lonely, and lovely soul who loved nature and animals and wanted to participate in life differently than anyone else. To this day we talk about you, your story. We wonder where you are and if you *made* it?

When you were with us, we were desperate to help fix the brokenness. Maybe we were all too desperate. When you talked, if you talked, you gave us very little. There wasn't a lot of substance. Was that just your way of interacting with the world or was the fault ours for not having enough experience to work with you? You were angry. You were angry because you wanted to go home, wanted your family back together, angry because you had to come visit us.

You could sound demented or sane, engaged, emotional, hollow, or tragically happy. You went to great lengths to control your world. You were also controlled by others and the situation. And truthfully you were, often, in control. Your eyes were dark, and behind your eyes was more darkness. You loved deeply those things you loved: your animals, your home, your abuser. You hated everyone and everything else. I think we tried to hear this but somehow none of us got your story right, did we?

We know you felt forced to tell who hurt you. You told us. We know you felt like we had taken away your family. You cried and screamed trying to tell us all how you felt. If you were to sit with us today, what would you ask? Would you ask why we didn't do more? Would you tell us we did more harm than good? Would you tell us to leave your family alone? Would you scream and tell us we stopped too soon? Do you know that we still mourn you? We grieve our decisions that lead to you not getting all the help that we think you needed. Maybe we were not the right place for you to get help and find your peace. Or maybe our picture of you was wrong.

Were we wrong? Did everyone get your story wrong? There is this confusing system that tries to help children. The system is multilayered, wrought with rules, and timelines filled with conflicting roles between agencies that just want to help. This system, with its created intention of good, is confusing even to us and we work in it every day. So many times we get it right. In those times, the child gets help and the perpetrator goes to prison. Or the parent gets help, gets off drugs and the family is stabilized. Not with you. We didn't help you. And as a system we were not at our best. You talked to too many people. We pushed. You retreated. You talked to law enforcement. You talked to child protective services. You talked to us. You talked to law enforcement again. You talked to child protective services again.

You talked to us a long time. There was never a time you were willing to make him the bad guy. You were unwilling to throw him away. The person who hurt you was also your protector. All the professionals had their own ideas regarding how to proceed. We wanted the person that hurt you to be punished. We wanted you to talk and heal. We wanted you to live away from the one home that you had always known. In our need to help we may have caused more pain. We thought you needed to feel safe, to tell "the truth." We chose to interpret your story. We lost you then. Maybe we lost you before you came to us. Maybe you would have never told your story. But we still feel responsible for the loss, for losing you, for you losing.

You are older now, gone from us, living your own life. All these years later, we still talk about you and wonder where you are in your life. Are you finding life difficult or have you become an adult that is thriving? We ask that you forgive us for being too caring, too inexperienced with your pain, and overeager in our need to help. We won't apologize for wanting to convict the person who hurt you. We will apologize for not understanding the extent to which you cared for that person. We think we have all the answers but we don't.

We help so many children but somehow could not help you. We have watched many children who experienced years of abuse by a parent, step-parent, or other close member of the family become thriving, happy, young adults. These children went through the whole awful experience of therapy, group, talking, crying, and in some cases testifying. The years of working through the emotions and learning to name the experience was long, but, in the end, helpful.

You were different. Your story was set to end in the manner it did. It was not the ending we imagined or wanted but it was your story, your ending. We think we looked too deeply, too quickly into your eyes and saw the pain you wanted to hide. It is hard to admit that we could have been wrong. There were times when you showed glimpses of another girl inside. Then again, it could have been your way of reminding us of what you wanted.

And if we are truthful, we could have created our own version of your story. As you shared photos, we saw a little girl with a sunny disposition. Maybe that was one moment in time. Maybe it was you before you came into our system. You showed a snapshot of a perfect little family. All we saw was the problem, not your family. Was this a pivotal moment? Did you use the photos to get our attention? Were you allowing glimpses into your life or were you saying get out of my life we are fine? Was that moment a façade or was that the real you? We still can't decide.

Regardless of the meaning that we got right or completely missed, our time together was a privilege. It was a gift. It felt big. We are thankful for you. You held up a mirror and showed us our flaws. We gasped in horror at our inadequacies. We defended our failures as someone else's fault. You forced us to look at the way we work. You forced us to work better together. This took some time, a long time. We had to step back to look at our failures. It is painful to admit failures. But in your story we found a better way. We did this slowly. Similar to the process of therapy, we would take pieces of this story and ask ourselves, "How do we do better?" You made us better.

In our haste to protect children we forgot that you were scared of losing someone you loved. You hurt on many levels and couldn't explain to us what it all meant. Or maybe we didn't listen closely enough to what you said. We focused only on the pain of that physical hurt and the one who hurt you. The hurt is always what we are eager to make right, to fix. But we couldn't fix you, could we? You were not a problem to be solved. We wanted to help fix your childhood but that wasn't our job. Our job is to stand by you and walk with you when you allow it. The person to put things right is the one you still love. As you continue to live in this world and make your own life, we have a few thoughts to take with you:

1. We are here. We will remain here, and if you need us you can call. Or call someone else. Just talk to someone. Find someone with whom you can share your pain. Allow someone to help you navigate through the pain and find resolution.
2. Grieve. It is important to cry. Cry about your life and your losses. Crying is not a weakness. It is a way our body releases emotions.

3. Get angry. Get angry and get better. Feel better. Don't do any of this because we told you to or because we want you to do so. Do it for yourself. Do it to prove you are better than your pain and hurt.

4. Learn to trust. There are people you can trust. Not everyone will hurt you or break your soul. Trust is a fragile thing. Maybe you can't trust us. We were the first to hear what happened. And maybe you can't forgive us for that. Maybe you won't forgive us for opening the wounds. Find someone else you in whom you can put your trust. In order to heal you might have to admit how much you hurt and how much you were hurt.

5. Learn to hope. Hope is a word sometimes misused and often used too much. Hope is intangible. But hope is also something larger than us. It is like a balloon. It can lift you to greater heights if you are willing to risk the possibility of falling when the balloon pops. There is nothing wrong with risk and failure, for only in those moments can we find our true selves and purpose. Hope gives us something to hold on to, a way around a difficult situation, some grace during our most difficult times. Don't give up. Grab hold and allow it to lift your spirits. Use hope to get you to the place you want to be.

6. Then there is *next*. Where do you go from here? The future is yours seems trivial. The future, like the world, is big and full of hopes and dreams. It can also be a scary place. There is this blank space in the future that no one but you can determine. You can't see the future so it can be a bit daunting to jump into life and find out what the future will bring. The future is a place where anything can happen, and yes, that means bad as well as good. But you can make your world into whatever you want. You are in charge of your next. Trust in the ability of your creative spirit to lead you to your future.

Your soul is beautiful. You were hurt but not broken. You have a life to lead that can go in many directions. You can choose to allow all this to define you, or you can choose to define yourself. Choose hope and living and next.

Andrea Gibby is the executive director and Natalie Whitehead is a clinical child therapist and forensic interviewer at the Appalachian Children's Center in Ellijay, Georgia.

CHAPTER 10

The Gift of Healing

Who doesn't love a present? Well, there may be some out there who don't, but most people do and we especially tend to appreciate a gift that is just what was wanted and needed. It could be that you never knew you wanted or needed a particular gift until someone who knows you well surprises you with the most precious of gifts, one that shows you that you are loved and cared for deeply by the giver. They know you. They get you and want you to see and feel that you are loved and understood. How wonderful! But there is another thing about a gift that is important to understand. There are secret powers in a gift that goes way beyond the good feeling when they are received. The benefit of a gift for the recipient can be quite obvious, but there is another facet of gift that is much more powerful.

What happens when you give a gift? Hopefully you have felt that special joy at Christmas or other holidays, on loved ones' birthdays, when marriages happen, babies are being born, all the times in our lives where gift giving occurs.

> *"There is a clear path to healing from any pain that is available to anyone. It begins with where your power truly lies. That place and that 'something' is you. The healing begins with you, but it is not really about you! That's the key, it is just the opposite."*

Think about how good you feel when you have given a gift that makes someone you care about happy. There are also the more unpleasant times when you realize your gift was a bit off the mark or not appreciated. So giving a gift to someone is an act that can produce some really good feelings for you, most of the time. But did you realize that giving in general was actually a powerful force in healing? It truly can when it is purposeful and done with love.

But that said, maybe you don't feel much in a mood to give. You have been hurt. Perhaps your child has been hurt. Your family has been hurt. We have all been hurt in our lives, but it could be that your current level of pain is of a magnitude that has turned all your thoughts inward. That is understandable. The levels of anyone's pain are their own at any moment in time and should always be respected. There are those who seem to bounce back quickly from hurt. There are those who turn to personally-destructive behaviors to block out the pain. There are those who do their best to distract themselves from their pain by substance abuse, various forms of criminal activity, or thoughts/acts of revenge that could also go as far as becoming a criminal act. Those choices never bring true peace. They most often lead to more sources for hurt in others and in the one who is initiating the act. These are not good paths toward healing.

The ultimate desperate release from pain for some people comes from suicide. When someone is in that deep place of hurt, their thoughts are not about others but only on themselves and what they have decided is the only path to relief. They sincerely do not believe or can't see that their healing is possible. They cannot seem to see or understand that the hurt they feel cannot be eased unless they are dead will just pass to all of those who love them; that their act will not only remove any chance of their healing but will forever transfer their hurt, magnified many times over, to their loved ones who will then themselves seek paths to healing. Suicide can often lead to more suicides by those who pattern themselves in seeking the path that someone they loved took. The good news is that not everyone who thinks about taking the path of suicide goes through with that choice. If they are fortunate to have someone with whom to share their thoughts, then help can be found. Belief in a higher power and petitions to that source have been answered and been a source of saving someone from that ultimate choice.

There are also the seemingly positive distractions people try in attempting to handle their emotional pain. Know any serious workaholics? There are other escape routes people attempt such as excessive television watching, movies, shopping, hobbies, video games, Facebook, exercise, and even church attendance. Then there is a real popular source of comfort, food. We all can indulge in some comfort eating from time to time, no harm, no foul. But . . . when food is your only source of pleasure and comfort then there just can't ever be enough, and next thing the person knows there are additional causes for pain as a result of excessiveness illness, disease and damage to your body that is difficult to take back. While indulging in many of these distracting or enjoyable activities can bring temporary relief, these are not the way to true long lasting healing. When all is said and done, you are back where you were before or worse. You might find yourself with a whole lot less money in the bank and finding you have clothes that no longer fit. That certainly won't make you feel better!

So what to do? Hurt from abusive behavior toward you and/or your loved is a big hit to take. Abusive hurt is always a part of you and changes you forever, but it does not have to define your life and rob you of ever having real happiness. Being hurt often means you feel powerless and maybe you are self-doubting. It may seem that you are haunted by feelings of guilt, blame, and "what ifs." Maybe you are at a point where you don't see good things ahead and it seems that your eyes have lost the ability to clearly see the beauty all around you and even the beauty that is inside of you. Maybe your personal hurt is so great that it does not seem you are ever meant to be happy again, but we beg to differ.

There is a clear path to healing from any pain that is available to anyone. It begins with where your power truly lies. That place and that "something" is you. The healing begins with you, but it is not really *about* you! That's the key, it is just the opposite. The instruction is simple: "Love one another." Take yourself out of the equation. *Lose yourself in your concern for others.* There is no room for depression, self-medication, anger, or judgment when you are focused on doing something kind for another person. Feeling good and happy is within your reach, but you must reach out. For your healing to begin, you do have to be active. You have to get up and plan each day to do something, anything, for someone else. It doesn't take money. You don't have to have any talents or special abilities. You don't have to get dressed up or be that smart. You don't have to ask permission or have a great plan.

You don't need to tell anyone at all. In fact, secret acts of compassion and kindness are the very best of all and have the greatest power there is to be produced.

The power of healing is very apparent in the work we see our volunteers give to our Children's Advocacy Center. People are touched by the pain and stress of children and families who have suffered family violence and child abuse. They want to DO something and seek our organization for ways they can help. The majority of those who come to us wanting to work for our programs as a volunteer have either been hurt themselves or have had someone close to them hurt as well. They find peace and healing in the varieties of activities and projects we offer volunteers. Here is a great example.

In 2015, our CAC offered a volunteer project that resulted in a powerful message of love at our facility. Volunteers were asked to support a project for a "happy fence." The decorative fence consists of wooden slats of varying height painted as children. The children on the fence represent all races and ethnicities. They are varying sizes and hold many different expressions. You can't help but smile at them and some are smiling back at you! The fence now lines the front walkway to our CAC ensuring that every child who enters knows as they walk to our door that they are valued and loved by those inside. They arrive to talk about a difficult experience but understand right away that it is a cheerful place where they are welcome.

As we began the "happy fence" project, it was a pleasure to see how many local community members were excited to be a part of the project whether they were artistically talented or not. One of those who painted six of the fence slats had a mother diagnosed with terminal cancer with just months to live. Another was someone whose husband had recently been diagnosed with Alzheimer's. Each one of these volunteers who painted for us brought their creations to us with huge smiles on their faces and left feeling good about knowing they had done something important for someone else, and it had made THEM feel awesome. This can be your feeling as well.

If you are a parent or caregiver of a child who has been abused, look for ways to give them the opportunity to do for others. If you are the one who is full of hurt and anger and pain, then the focus is on you to find a way to give. In your everyday life there are many chances to be kind to people. Look around you and where you live. To help generate your production of ideas that would work for you, here is a list of kind deeds to consider. You could do these alone or with children, depending on your children and the activity, of course.

o   Take some food and a blanket to your local animal shelter and love on some future pets.

o   On Mother's or Father's Day, take a homemade card to someone who has lost their parent recently.

o   "Adopt" someone in a nursing home who is a shut-in and visit with a drawing made just for them. If you hit it off, plan to visit them regularly, especially during and on holidays.

o   Join a group who is doing an Adopt-a-Mile clean-up project.

o   Offer to take a buggy back in the store for someone who is finished shopping.

o   Decide to just walk around the parking lot putting up buggies that others leave all over the place!

o   *(You may have realized the author has a pet peeve on shopping lot buggy abandonment.)*

o   Plant a garden and then share your produce with someone you don't even know.

o   When you hear the sirens of ambulance and/or fire trucks, say a quiet prayer for the safety of all concerned.

o   Offer to take out your neighbor's trash . . . or just do it secretly!

o   Speaking of your neighbor, how about going out one day and picking up sticks and/or pine cones for them, raking up some straw, gathering some flowers?

o   Start collecting canned goods and personally deliver at local food bank.

o   At Christmastime, sign up to ring the Salvation Army bell.

o   In the check-out line, give a compliment to the person at the register, with a big smile.

Starting now, look out each day for some small ways you can do something for someone. Embrace those outside your family and friend circles and make a stranger's day with your kindness. As your children watch you they learn and become themselves active in healing their own hurts. Everyone feels good inside. Everyone realizes just how strong and powerful they are in their ability to help others. Everyone heals.

Take back your life from any hurt that controls you and then pay it forward in active love for others. Relax and enjoy the peace, joy, beauty, and healing that grows within as a result. Please share your experiences of healing as we know they will happen for you, and then all of a sudden, there you are, a healer yourself! One more thing, don't stop once you start to feel some peace. Make a conscious choice to be sure to do at least one kind thing for a stranger, a neighbor, anyone every day. Be grateful for all you have that brings you joy. Be the joy for others and before you know it, that joy in your own heart has replaced the hurt, anger, and loss that used to reign.

Peace be with you always.

Nancy Bryan is the executive director of Ruth's Cottage and The Patticake House in Tifton, Georgia.

CHAPTER 11

Healing Shouldn't Hurt—The Medical Exam

"Hi, my name is Heather. I'll be doing the medical exam today." "Oh, okay . . . well, is anything hurting on you today, Jane?" "Okay, Mom . . . I need some information on Jane's health before this exam and just so you understand, the medical exam is much like an exam at the doctor's office. It's not too invasive but it can be stressful. I will need you to sign here to release this information to the detective in your case." "Okay, let's get started."

First of all, child abuse should not happen. It does though, as we know. And, when it does, it puts into motion a lifetime of ripple effects. Abuse affects the brain, the body, and the soul of its victim. Trauma can manifest into physical symptoms and mental disorders that cause lifelong problems, so when it occurs there is often evidence that needs to be collected both physically and "mentally" in the form of the verbal disclosure.

I'm a science person. Even more, I'm a science-minded person who enjoys children much more than

> *"For a split second, I wanted to cry. I wanted to cry at the absolute fear and isolation that Jane must have felt for all of those years thinking that she—and only she—might be the only child on the planet that is so terrible that she must deserve being sexually abused by her own caregiver. I wanted to cry for the survivors still out there who might feel this way now. The relief in her eyes when she realized that this was not and is not the truth will remain an unforgettable image for me."*

adults in nearly every setting and situation. For this reason, I pursued a career in pediatrics and forensic medicine and have spent the last twenty years providing forensic medical examinations and health care to young people. This is what is commonly known as the "rape exam" or the "forensic medical exam or S.A.N.E." In an average year, our child advocacy center will conduct around one hundred forensic medical examinations on children that have experienced physical or sexual assault. For me, I have conducted around 450 medical examinations on children and adolescents over the last eighteen years.

For the majority of medical examinations, there is a rigid process of examining the body to collect evidence and document any findings. Sometimes lab work and photography is involved and in some rare occasions it is not. The developmental age of a child is also a huge factor in how the examination is done and can be a factor in the emotional response. Depending on the age of the child or adolescent, the examination can be very difficult physically. But, in every case, I believe that the examination is extremely stressful for any age. In fact—and this is my own unproven and unresearched opinion—it seems that the older the victim perhaps the more stressful emotionally it is for them.

Not every case of abuse has to have a medical exam, but oftentimes it can really help. Not only can medical exams document any injuries or illnesses for evidence collection, but very often the examination itself can provide reassurance to the child that their body is okay and "just like everyone else's." Most experts agree that molecular evidence (DNA) begins to degenerate within seventy-two hours after an assault, leaving traces of forensic evidence difficult to collect after such time has elapsed. Physical injuries to skin such as bruising and lacerations can also be difficult to assess or properly identify after several days. In children, the rate of tissue repair and healing is faster, making the collection of physical evidence from assaults in child victims even harder.

For the most part, the forensic medical exam is much like a head-to-toe exam that a child would experience at a pediatrician's office. Aside from collecting any evidence, the medical exam is assessing for any injury, disease, or illness that may need treatment, and providing reassurance to the child and their caregiver that all is well from a medical health care perspective. It is not uncommon for lab work and cultures to be obtained even if many years have passed after the alleged assault. It is also not uncommon to not find any abnormal changes or injuries in children even after suffering years of abuse. In fact, almost all statistics support that no physical evidence will be found in 85 percent of all cases of sexual abuse. This is largely due to the fact that the body heals and heals itself very well—especially in children. The presence or absence of menstruation in female survivors impacts the appearance of the genital tissue that are examined which can cause injuries sustained in childhood from being visible later on. With all this being said, the important thing to understand about the medical examination is that it is primarily done to assess for injuries and illnesses that may need medical attention or documentation and to reassure the child that they are going to be okay. Not finding evidence to support the child's disclosure is not reason to disbelieve them, it is simply a very unusual thing to find in even the most gruesome cases of abuse.

It is not uncommon for the medical exam to be an emotionally stressful event for the child and their caregiver. Even though the medical exam is similar to a "well child" exam that they may have experienced before, being undressed and touched by anyone, even a health care provider, can cause a great deal of anxiety. Examining the genitals (the "private parts") is nearly always the last part of the exam because it is the most invasive part which causes the greatest amount of stress both physically and emotionally—to the child and the examiner to be honest.

The medical examination can prove to be a great comfort to survivors. It can reassure them that their body is healthy, free of disease or injury, or simply to know that they "look normal" when trauma can create a sense that you are anything but normal although the vast majority of medical examinations do not have any physical findings such as DNA, evidence of injury, or even abnormal scarring or such changes. This is very often difficult for nonmedical people to understand.

Over the last eighteen years, several children have made lasting impressions on me. In one case of extreme physical abuse, I examined a child that had sustained more injuries in the form of broken bones, bruises, and lacerations across her entire body than most people might have over their lifetime. Her examination was unforgettable to me, not because of the injuries but because of her smiling. This child smiled during her entire exam. She told me that she was so happy that she was getting "checked out" because she hurt all over and was scared something was "bad wrong" with her.

As I measure and photograph an injury, I often ask a child how it happened. Sometimes they do not remember and oftentimes they do. This particular child was able to describe not only the severe injuries that were present during this exam but she also described very similar previous episodes of repeated abuse leaving her with similar pain. Even in her pain that day, she described a "worse time" of severe physical abuse. As we finished up the exam, I was explaining how we would get the x-rays and follow-up care she was going to need. After being so happy during the exam, her smile faded and she asked me if her dad would go to jail for hurting her. I told her that I was not the one that made that decision but my job was to evaluate her health. Then, I thanked her for her cooperation and amazing patience with me, as her exam took several hours. She hugged me, said she understood that I couldn't answer her question. But she went on to tell me that although she knew what her father had done to her was wrong, she was going to heal and eventually be okay and she did not want to cause any problems for her family. She told me that she could endure the pain and knew she would heal, but her family needed their dad. This child was twelve years old. She had sustained physical abuse for years and she still smiled when anyone was nice to her. It occurred to me that children do not want to hurt their families. And, they definitely do not want to be the source of trouble for them, even if it causes them suffering.

As I reviewed my case for the months following, I was continuously reminded of her strength for every photograph I had taken of her injured body during the examination; she was smiling so big I could see her teeth. A "toothy smile" is what we call that in my family. She smiled a "toothy smile." A beaten twelve-year-old child with more forgiveness and love in her than most adults can display reminds me of the strength of all children.

One of the most unforgettable moments for me several years ago was a young girl who was less than ten years old who had disclosed being sexually abused by her stepfather for approximately three years. Let's call the child "Jane." We began the exam in the usual fashion—listen to the heart, the lungs, looked at the outside of the body in a slow manner to assess for injuries moving toward the final stages of the exam. So, as I continued to examine the outside of Jane's body, we had some simple conversation. Typically, when a child has already disclosed abuse to another professional or had a forensic interview, I avoid any direct questioning about the abuse to avoid re-traumatizing the child and possibly contaminating any previous disclosure. I like to talk to the child about things he/she enjoys.

Jane and I were having a nice conversation about her school friends when out of the blue, Jane asked me if I did "this kind of thing a lot" (examine children who had been sexually abused). I replied, "Well, yes. I am looking for any injuries that might need medicine and making sure that your body is in perfect health. I do it for all of the kids that come here. This is what we do here." Jane could not believe it, and when she told me that she thought she was the only person it happened to, I stood there frozen.

Now, I think most of the professionals that I work with who are involved in investigating child abuse cases and treating child abuse victims would agree that most victims feel that their abuse is embarrassing to discuss. Almost all victims feel the elements of shame and isolation. These emotions that victims might express are the subject of many training classes that most of us in the field of treating abuse survivors learn about. And, for some strange reason, Jane's very honest and very simple statement that she was shocked to hear that some other child might possibly be abused just like her made my stomach grip. I think I even stared blankly back and said, "Of course! I work with tons of kids that have been abused just like you." Now, I am certain that a lot of children who have been in this situation have felt this exact emotion and probably even had this realization before when coming to the advocacy center. Even after learning in class after class that survivors may feel alone or experience isolation, I still just couldn't believe my ears. To make the situation even more profound for me was the pure look of relief and joy in Jane's eyes as she realized that yes, yes, there are kids just like her who are sexually abused. And, she knows it is true because here is this whole big house and exam room dedicated to listening to them, examining their bodies, and praising them for their survival. For a split second, I wanted to cry. I wanted to cry at the absolute fear and isolation that Jane must have felt for all of those years thinking that she—and only she—might be the only child on the planet that is so terrible that she must deserve being sexually abused by her own caregiver. I wanted to cry for the survivors still out there who might feel this way now.

The relief in her eyes when she realized that this was not and is not the truth will remain an unforgettable image for me. No, Jane, you are not the only child being abused, and for that, I am very, very sorry. And I am so honored to be able to provide you with care and a place to begin healing as you begin to try and understand why. I know Jane is a survivor, but I got to see her strength turn into joy when she realized that she was not alone—there are others just like her. Her excited smile is the other image that I will never forget.

I am often asked how I do "this work," and I really think that Jane's smile of relief might be one of the main reasons. Child abuse should not happen. But it does. And when it does, it puts into motion a lifetime of ripple effects. Those ripples affect far more than the victims and their families. They affect whole communities and shape the world as a whole. It is an honor and a blessing to be able to do "this work" and, when possible, change the direction of those painful ripples to ones of healing.

Heather Hayes is the executive director of the Edmondson-Telford Center for Children in Gainesville, Georgia.

CHAPTER 12

What am I Doing Here? A Practical Chapter of Advice and Encouragement

So here you sit, picking up this book that has been given to you, and not really knowing if it is going to be helpful at all. You are probably asking yourself, *"What am I doing here? How did we get to this place?"* Well, we might not have the answers to those big questions but we do have important messages that we want to send your way. Glance through the chapter at the headings. See if any of the topics grab you. Read the sections that catch your eye. We hope these words help you heal. I wrote this as if I was sitting down beside you, looking you in the eye, and sharing what I know.

Do Not Blame Yourself
As a caregiver, it's easy to blame yourself for what happened to your child. Think about it like this: a tornado hitting your house (you might kind of feel that way, huh?). You would never want that to happen any more than you'd want your child to be hurt. You can go over in your head well before the storm clouds form, how you would react, and "prepare," but there is nothing you can do to prevent that tornado from hitting your house. Right now, you are just coming out to see the destruction that has been left behind. It is overwhelming. Just know that you are having a normal response to something that is very unusual for you. True, your life and your child's life will never be the same. But there is HOPE. With time, help, and "clean up," your life (and your child's life) will get back to a "normal" routine. Will you or your child ever be the same again? No. Will you and your child recover and become stronger in some ways? *YES! You will do it together. And you will be surrounded by people to show you the way.*

Why didn't my child tell as soon as this happened?

Sometimes kids don't tell about what happened to them for a long time, and some children never tell. Sometimes they don't tell everything that has happened to them. Telling takes time. It is painful, like having a splinter in your finger and trying to get it out. Here is a good way to explain it: how does it feel when you have the splinter in your finger (not telling certain things)? It hurts. How does it feel when you're getting the splinter out of your finger (talking about what happened)? It REALLY hurts! How does it feel once the splinter is out (once you've told what happened to you and how scared you are)? It starts to feel better. What happens if you don't tell (keep it on the inside)? It gets infected. We don't want that. Telling is hard. But with help from family, friends, and time, kids can heal.

Your child's thoughts, feelings, and fears

Kids feel all kinds of feelings about what happened to them. They have all different thoughts about the person who hurt them, themselves, and what happened to them. They might feel mad, sad, betrayed, embarrassed, scared, and many other things. Remember: whatever your child is thinking and feeling is *normal*. Remind your child of that often. And remind yourself. And don't ever forget about the importance of counseling . . . there are great people out there who you and your child can talk to and who can help you sort through those thoughts, feelings, and fears.

Only one person is responsible!

There is one person responsible for what happened. The offender. Don't beat yourself over the head with coulda' shoulda' woulda'. The "best" parents/caregivers in the world have found themselves in your situation (remember the tornado analogy?). Would you blame yourself for a tornado hitting your house? No. Then why are you blaming yourself for what happened with your child? Blame gets in the way of healing.

Keep talking to your child

Make sure to keep talking to your child about all kinds of things. For example, make sure you are talking to your child about body safety. Maybe you have done some of this over the years, but maybe you haven't. Just know that it's never too late to start. We always suggest starting simple when they are young and then adding a little more information each year. Meaning when they are two to three years old, you talk about how it's not okay for someone to touch the parts of their body that are covered by a swimming suit. Then as they get to age four and five, you talk in more detail about what we call "uh-oh" touches and how important it is to tell a trusted adult when they get a bad feeling or are uncomfortable around someone. You will find that as your child gets older, if you have been really open and available to talk about this uncomfortable subject, it will get easier. At all ages, it is always a great idea to use "what would you do if . . ." with them to see how they would handle different situations. You can use this to find out all kinds of things from what they would do if a friend wanted them to steal some candy at the store all the way to how they would handle a situation where someone touches them inappropriately. The goal is to make sure that they know they can come to you to talk about ANYTHING.

Recovering from this . . . will it ever happen?

Yes! Your recovery (and your child's recovery) will have good days, better days, and worse days . . . like a roller-coaster ride. At the end of your healing journey, you will get back to a happy "normal" life. A good day might be a day that you actually don't think about what happened that brought you to this place. Maybe your child brings home an unexpected great score on a spelling test and you take him out for a surprise scoop of ice cream. Or maybe a good day is when your child's therapist lets you know that she feels that she just needs to see your child on an as-needed basis since things seem to be going well. But a "worse day" might be one where you feel like you are alone on this journey and you don't seem to have any other caregivers to talk to who can relate to what you and your child are going through. On those days, you need to pick up the phone and call the Children's Advocacy Center where you and your child were served and ask them for some direction. That's what they are there for, to connect you to support and services on those "worse days." You might not be comfortable asking for help or admitting that you or your child is struggling, but it's more important now than ever to ask for that help, so that you all can recover and heal.

Testing limits

Your child may "test limits" to see what he or she can get away with after he or she discloses. It may seem like they are using the abuse as an excuse to misbehave. That's normal. Some degree of "rebellion" or "temper tantrums" or "bad days" are part of the healing process. Keep that in the back of your mind. Consider it. Still enforce the house rules and the schedules that you had before the disclosure.

Allow your child to talk to their siblings

Some parents try to keep one child's abuse a secret from the other children in the home. Those brothers and sisters know more about the situations than we think. A cookie-cutter approach does not work with this. Discuss your particular situation with professionals. Also talk to your child to find out their comfort level when it comes to how much they want their siblings to know. Many times kids want to have control of when and how others find out about their abuse. Remember: your family is on this journey together. When one child is abused, if affects all of you.

Nothing changed ... EVERYTHING changed

It's as simple as that. Some days it is as if nothing has changed. Other days it seems like EVERYTHING in your life has changed. Remember, what happened to your child doesn't define who your child is. AND what happened to your child doesn't define who you are. We know you feel like your whole life has turned . . . or turned upside down or backward . . . but keep walking . . . keep moving forward, not just for your child but for yourself.

Take care of you!

During this journey, make yourself a priority. Take care of you! It is not selfish. You are finding out how to stay strong for the journey. It is necessary. When you are feeling overwhelmed and sad, take a quiet moment to yourself . . . and just breathe. Don't beat yourself up. Move forward.

You can do this!

You are so much stronger than you think you are. Really, you are! We know you don't want to be in this situation . . . you might be saying, "Why me? Why us? Why our family?" Remember: you can take this journey with your child! Your child needs you leading the way! Hold your head high! You've got this! You won't feel like you do. BUT. . . every day, every hour, every minute, you are the most important person in your child's life! So . . . for your child. . . YOU'VE GOT THIS!

Being scared does not mean you are weak!

Really . . . fear isn't weakness. It's human nature to be scared in situations like this. Listen again to that statement: *being scared does not mean you are weak*. It just means that you are scared. You can be courageous *and* strong during scary times. You've done it before in all kinds of situations with your child.

Identify "rescuers"

Okay, by this we mean find people who can walk this journey with you, who can support you and encourage you. Yes, this means you will need to tell them about the situation you and your child are in. You need people to "rescue" you from your fear and self-doubting. Asking for help when you need it and asking someone to rescue you when you need it is a *brave* thing to do.

Forgive yourself

You might be saying, "No way! That's not happening!" Well, at least put it on your to-do list as you walk this journey. Really . . . consider forgiving yourself as a caregiver/parent. Be present with your child now. Be protective of your child NOW! Don't look back. You can be paralyzed by "what if I had . . ."

And finally, PRAISE YOUR CHILD!

Our kids can NEVER get enough praise from us, right? We all like hearing that we are great. So, now more than ever. . . praise your child. Be specific. Instead of saying, "You are great" and "I love you so much," try saying some of these:

ALWAYS KNEW YOU COULD DO IT. NOW YOU'RE FLYING. NOW YOU'VE GOT IT. YOU'RE ON YOUR WAY. YOU'RE BEAUTIFUL. YOU'RE UNIQUE. NOTHING CAN STOP YOU NOW. BEAUTIFUL

WORK. DREAM BIG! SPECTACTULAR. **I BELIEVE YOU.** FABULOUS. TREMENDOUS. YOU'RE IMPORTANT. VERY CREATIVE. **YOU'RE SO RESPONSIBLE.** WHAT AN IMAGINATION. I'M PROUD OF YOU. YOU'RE REALLY GROWING UP. YOU ARE SUCH A GOOD FRIEND. I TRUST YOU. YOU'RE IMPORTANT. YOU MEAN A LOT TO ME. YOU MAKE ME LAUGH. YOU BRIGHTEN MY DAY. I RESPECT YOU. YOU MEAN THE WORLD TO ME. YOU'RE A JOY. YOU'RE A TREASURE. YOU'RE SPECTACULAR. THAT WAS VERY THOUGHTFUL. TERRIFIC.

So… we want to close our chapter with a cliché. Here it is:

HANG IN THERE!

Stand as strong as you can, hug your kids tight, tell them you believe in them, and keep walking. YOU'VE GOT THIS!

Gail Garland is a former executive director of Harbor House, the Child Advocacy Center, in Rome Georgia.

CHAPTER 13

You're Our Hero!

For young kids:

Thanks for coming to see us today! We know it wasn't easy. You were probably pretty nervous and maybe even a little scared about coming to the center to talk about all that stuff—but you did great!

We are all so proud of you!

Do you know what courage is? Real courage is when you're afraid to do something, but you know that it's really important, so in spite of being scared, you just go ahead and DO it. And that's what you did today! You were scared to talk about all that stuff, but you did it anyway.

Maybe you thought you were in trouble, or that no one would believe you, or that it was somehow your fault . . . but by being so brave and using your voice, you found out that just the opposite was true. You know now that you aren't in trouble, and we DO believe you, and that it wasn't your fault . . . not one bit. Now you know that when a grown-up or bigger kid forces or tricks a younger kid into sexual touching, it's NEVER the younger kid's fault.

"And you know that you have friends at the center who will always be here if there is something you need to talk about—or just to check in and say hi."

Now you know how important it is to use your voice and to talk to trusted adults when something is bothering you or just doesn't feel right. And you know that you have friends at the center who will always be here if there is something you need to talk about—or just to check in and say hi.

So keep in touch with us, okay? And keep being brave!

<u>For parents of young kids</u>:

Thanks for bringing your child to talk with us today. We know it was almost as scary for you as it was for your child. But s/he learned today that there are adults that s/he can trust and rely on, that will believe what s/he has to say, and help you take the appropriate steps for your family.

We are here for you whenever you need us. We hope you'll follow up with counseling for your child, either here at the center, or, if you prefer, in the community. Because we have such great therapists and such a well-stocked play therapy room, kids usually want to return to the center—and they always get a great deal out of their sessions here. We'll also be here for your child throughout the criminal justice process, to help inform and advocate, and at any time in the future that we may be needed.

We're here for you, as well, to provide whatever resources and support you may need. Please feel free to call on us, particularly when you're feeling down or depressed or overwhelmed.

And remember: with your support, your child is going to be just fine, even if s/he does go through some rough patches in the weeks ahead. You may even be surprised that s/he seems to be doing as well as s/he is—but that's in large part due to YOUR support. When parents believe their kids and let them know that they're believed, and when they take steps to protect children and to cooperate with the investigation and prosecution, then kids get the message that telling was the right thing to do. And they come to understand that if something bad happens in the future, they can trust their parents to believe and support them.

Today your child learned to use her voice . . . and you both learned that we're here when you need us.

<u>For older kids</u>:

We know you must have been nervous about coming here today and having to talk about all that stuff. You may feel like this kind of thing doesn't happen to other people—but it does. It happens a LOT: one in four girls and one in six boys will be sexually abused before the age of 18. Think about how many people in your class, let alone your school, that means have been through the same kind of thing you have. The only difference is that you were brave enough to tell, so congratulations! You should be really proud of yourself!

You probably have a lot of questions about what comes next and what will happen in the future. We'll do our best to answer your concerns as they come up, so never be embarrassed about calling (or having your mom or dad call) to ask us any questions that arise. For now, here are some of the concerns other young people have expressed:

What now? Good question but sometimes kind of hard to predict.

The first thing that had to happen was for you to be interviewed here at the advocacy center. Next, the detective will talk to anyone else who might have information or who might know about other kids the suspect (as the police call him) might have molested. If you had a medical exam, the detective will have to get a copy of the report. If you mentioned any particular items in your interview that can help to provide corroboration (the legal term for support) for your statement (pictures or text messages, for example), s/he will have to try to get those, as well. We're sorry, but that means you may have to give up your phone, your tablet, or even some of your clothes for a while. You will get them back but probably not right away.

Lots of people worry about court, but try not to. For one thing, most of our cases don't go to court—not because everyone doesn't believe the kid but just because there's not enough evidence (information that helps to prove the case) to go to trial. Sometimes it takes another kid getting brave enough to come forward before a case can go to court.

But just so you know, court is nothing like what you see on TV; it's much more boring and drawn out and less dramatic. Also, the attorney for the suspect (who in court is called the defendant) often gets very angry and blustery with witnesses (people who are giving evidence or who are testifying) on TV shows, but that's just TV. In real life, the defense attorney is usually pretty nice to kids; otherwise, the jury (the people who listen to the case and decide if the defendant is guilty or not) will think he's a big jerk, and hate him AND the defendant.

Another reason not to worry about court is that it takes a LONG time for a case to come to trial here, and in our courts we try to keep kids out as much as possible. That's one reason why the suspect may not be arrested right away; instead, child abuse cases are presented in supersecret hearings to twenty-three people called a Grand Jury. No one has to be there but the detective and the prosecutor (that's the lawyer for the state—because it's not you or your folks who are pressing charges against the suspect, it's the whole state of Georgia that is!). After the Grand Jury meets, the suspect may be arrested, but it will probably be another year until trial, and in the meantime—or even at the last minute—he could decide to plead guilty, so there would be no trial.

You may also be worried about your family, and that situation is even harder to predict—especially if it was a close relative or friend who was the molester. Family members may get upset, may be angry or sad, even seem depressed—but it's important to remember that YOU are not the cause of that because you did nothing wrong. The molester is the one who broke the law, who took advantage of your trust, and who is the cause of any distress in the family. All you did was tell the truth, which was the absolute right thing to do. Sometimes that might be hard to remember, but just keep in mind: if you saw a friend of yours rob a store, and you called 911, and he got in trouble, was that your fault? Of course not! You were just being a good citizen; HE is the one who broke the law. And just as with your situation, it's the person who did the wrong thing—not the one who told—who's responsible for whatever fallout occurs afterward.)

You may be worried about yourself, as well, and whether the sexual abuse has changed who you are forever. The answer is NO. Lots of things in your world may have changed, and aspects of your personality or behavior may have changed too: you may not trust people as much, you might feel fearful around men, you might be less outgoing and friendly or more jumpy and nervous. But those things don't make up who you are; they're feelings and behaviors that can change over time.

Counseling can really help—as it can with any other problems you may be experiencing as a result of what happened to you. Because the sexual abuse doesn't define you, it isn't who you are. It was a terrible and unfair thing that happened to you, but you survived. You're a survivor! And you're our hero!

For foster parents and kinship caregivers:

You already know that if a child has been placed in your home due to sexual abuse, it means the child's primary caretaker is either unable or unwilling to believe the allegations and protect the child. This makes your job as a caregiver even more difficult, because this lack of support and belief represents a double betrayal for the child—first by the offender and then by the parent who failed to provide protection from him.

We urge you to take advantage of counseling services at the CAC in your area, to bring the child consistently, and to follow up on suggestions made by the therapist. Kids in your care have suffered so much inconsistency, pain, and secret-keeping that it will probably take weeks of consistent therapy sessions before they are willing to begin opening up in therapy. During this time, it is important that you keep in touch with the therapist and let her know what you're seeing at home or what teachers are reporting to you about behavior at school.

Some kids will act out from the first day they're placed with relatives or foster parents. They test every limit, push every button. They're angry and hurt—and justifiably, because the parent who should have cared for and protected them has sided with the offender, and as a result, they have been placed out of their home. Being consistent with rules and schedules will help, as will unconditional acceptance of who they are (though not necessarily how they behave). They may have had too much control in their own homes and too few rules: they ate nothing but junk food, stayed up watching TV until they fell asleep, slept in if mom didn't get them up for school. Now they're being expected to follow rules and learn structure—and they'll fight back against both. Maintaining patience and predictability is crucial—don't allow yourself to be drawn into arguments or power struggles over violations of rules or consequences for those violations. (You won't win, and you'll both end up frustrated.)

On the other hand, during the first few weeks after placement, you may experience a "honeymoon" period with children. They may be surprisingly cooperative, agreeable, and helpful, seemingly fine despite the trauma they have suffered. So, when after a few weeks or even months, they become angry, defiant, rebellious, even destructive, you may be tempted to blame it on therapy. You may think that counseling is reopening old wounds, and raking them raw. You may believe that it's better to leave the past in the past, and behave as if all that old trauma and hurt aren't there.

But that is the worst thing we can do for kids. They need to be able to face their pain and work through it, so they don't carry it around for the rest of their lives. And they need to know that even at their very worst, they're still accepted and loved—and that you'll be there for them in a way that their biological parents weren't.

Many kids who've been abused, especially oldest children, may behave like parents toward their younger siblings. They may try to take charge of feeding, bathing, diapering, even discipline of the little ones—and it may cause great anxiety to them if you try to intervene. That was their function at home and often their only sense of self-worth. Even though it may be easier for you to let them continue to take charge, it is imperative that you not give in to that impulse. Kids NEED to be kids, and they need to know that you're an adult who can take care of them—and their younger sibs. It will be a tug of war for a while, but again consistency at home and counseling by a trained expert are key.

Let us know if we can help—and thanks for the dedication and compassion you showed by opening your home to children in need of nurture and stability.

Kris Rice is the former and founding executive director of the Coastal Children's Advocacy Center in Savannah, Georgia.

CHAPTER 14

Small But Precious Wonder-Filled Gifts

The young hatchling scurried across the golden grains of sand lighted by the very first rays of a new day's sunrise. The hatchling was on his way to the vastness of the Atlantic Ocean to face many challenges, but just the fact that he survived his first fifty-five to sixty-five days in the nest where his mother had carefully chosen to lay eggs was one of nature's miracles. This new hatchling survived many different predators such as raccoons and humans who made their way along the shore when it was in the nest. He shed his protective shell and began a relatively short trek to the ocean eager to embark on his own amazing journey. This baby loggerhead turtle was strong, resilient, and a survivor; loggerhead turtles have to be strong and resilient because only one hatchling in one thousand survives and make it to adulthood.

When a loggerhead turtle embarks on his journey through life, it is only about two inches in size. This very small but wonderful creature immediately heads in the direction of the brightest horizon, typically toward the ocean, when it hatches. Despite its small size and his vulnerability, the loggerhead turtle is believed to have survived for as long as two hundred million years. Yet despite its ability to survive for millions of years, due to many

"Children who have an adult in their life who is supportive and believes their disclosure respond better to therapy and cope better in their healing process than children who do not have the support of a loving and nurturing caregiver. Children also do not need to be blamed for the abuse they experienced."

predators such as pollution, shrimp trawling, coastal development, and even plastic bags, the loggerhead turtle was identified as threatened and placed on U.S. Federal Endangered Species list in 1978.

When I first saw the photograph of the baby loggerhead turtle in an art store, I was drawn to it, so much that I just had to purchase it. For me, this was not simply a photograph of a loggerhead turtle but instead it served as a summation of my beliefs and my hope for the children and families that I have been fortunate to serve throughout the years. Children, who despite the many difficult challenges they have suffered due to abuse and trauma have now become survivors and not victims of their circumstances. Children are very resilient and learn to thrive despite the vulnerability of their victimization. Like the loggerhead turtle hatchling, children must face the challenges of finding their way in turbulent and dangerous waters, to learn to live happy and healthy lives.

Child abuse is in no way a new issue in our society. Although new advances in technology such as the internet, smart phones, computers, and the like have emerged to make life easier, it has certainly created new risk factors for children than most would not have dreamed of twenty-five years ago. By 1967, child abuse reporting laws existed in all fifty states. And in 1974, only four years prior to loggerhead turtles being added to the threatened species list, the Federal Child Abuse and Neglect Prevention and Treatment Act went into effect and created prevention information to help adults become more aware of the need to recognize and report child abuse and better understand the long-term impact of abuse on children.

One of the first words that comes to my mind when I think about the children I have worked with during the past twenty-six years who have experienced sexual, physical, or emotional abuse and other traumas is RESILIENT. While children are often resilient, their resiliency does not eliminate the sometimes life-altering negative impact of the abuse or trauma they experienced. Despite the negative circumstance and the traumatic experiences children encounter, they develop ways to cope with the abuse they experience. Children try to engage in normal childhood activities; they try to focus on school and do their best to maintain their grades. They smile when they are terrified of being abused again on a new day and they even continue to love the people who have abused them, the very same people who they should be able to rely on to protect them and care for them. Children remain focused despite experiencing a sleepless night due to nightmares and difficult days at school due to many distractions and worries. Resiliency takes on many faces during the life of a child who is a victim of abuse or who witnesses domestic violence in their home.

Children who have experienced abuse or trauma, like the children we work with at a child advocacy center, often present symptoms. Some children present with one or two symptoms and sometimes other children present many symptoms that may affect their sleep patterns, eating habits, progress in the school setting, friendship/other relationships, physical health, or mental health. Many times a child may have symptoms, but the underlying cause of the symptoms remains unknown at times because often children do not immediately report the abuse they experience for weeks, months, or even years later. It is not unusual for children not to report the abuse they experienced as a child and they may not report even well into adulthood.

Often, while conducting an in-take with a child's parent(s), we learn that the child's parent was the victim of childhood abuse or trauma. Through the years, parent after parent have disclosed their own personal history of childhood abuse. Unfortunately, far too often the common thread we hear is that the parent told a trusted adult about being abused. Some adults will share that they were not believed when they disclosed their abuse. Others share that nothing was done when they disclosed about the abuse they experienced. Many report the abuse continued after they disclosed. And sadly, most adults report that they never received help or support after turning to a trusted adult to protect them from the abuse they were experiencing. Most parents experiencing abuse NEVER received services or support from a children's advocacy center.

At times, these adult survivors of childhood abuse express that they are grateful that things have changed and their child and family will have the opportunity to receive the help and support they never had access to. Other parents state, in a matter-of-fact voice of experience, that they survived without being believed or receiving counseling services and they are reluctant to access therapy and services for their children. At times, parents reveal their vulnerability and share how their child's victimization is "triggering" their own past abuse history and how difficult these feelings that resurface are for them. They are accepting of support not only their children, but they also take a risk and request support for themselves to finally begin to deal with many years of secrecy and bottled-up pain from their childhood. At times the parent's adult life mirrors a list of symptoms consistent with the childhood abuse they experienced: difficulty with relationships, addiction issues, eating issues, cutting, and mental health issues such as depression and anxiety. For most, the resources and services the parents learn about at a child advocacy center become a ray of hope not only for their child but for the family as well. Families learn, sometimes for the first time, that the cycle of abuse or what has become a multigenerational pattern of abuse in some families can come to an end.

As part of the closing stage of forensic interviews, children are asked to identify adults who they trust and know that they may go to if they need help or if they find themselves in a situation where someone is hurting them or they are afraid. I feel a sense of relief when children are able to name at least one trusted adult in their life. It is always good to hear children who can easily identify multiple adults who they trust enough to go to for help. I also try to make certain that children feel they know someone outside of their home that they may turn to as well. Often, children identify teachers, principals, nurses, counselors, doctors, and police officers. One of the concerning things I hear children say is that they do not have anyone that they can talk with or tell if they need to reach out for help in a situation. It is heartbreaking hearing a child say that they do not feel that they have at least one reliable, dependable, trusted adult in their life that they could turn to for help if ever needed.

Children need at least one reliable, dependable, trusted adult in their lives, someone who is nonjudgmental and that will truly listen to their concerns. Children need an adult who believes them and believes in them. Children need an adult who is supportive and protective. Children who have an adult in their life who is supportive and believes their disclosure respond better to therapy and cope better in their healing process than children who do not have the support of a loving and nurturing caregiver. Children also do not need to be blamed for the abuse they experienced.

It is my hope that this will be one of the living legacies of Children's Advocacy Centers. I hope children who experience abuse or trauma will be able to say, *"I went to this place and they listened to me. I was heard. I received help and support. My parent(s) received support and guidance. While we were hurting, my family is now stronger and I know what to do and have someone to tell if anyone ever tries to hurt me again."* I hope that no child will ever believe that they do not have a trusted adult that they can turn to for help.

I also hope the long-term legacy of Children's Advocacy Centers will be that children do not ever have to experience revictimization. I hope that the children whose lives we touch learn to cope and move on from the abuse and traumas they experienced. Children deserve opportunities to thrive and lead healthy, happy childhoods that grow into healthy, productive, and happy adulthoods. I hope that because of the services available at children's advocacy centers, the children we work with will become parents who are available and protective of their own children. While I am not naïve enough to believe that I will have to find a new line of work because child abuse is completely eradicated, I do hope that the work we do will significantly contribute to breaking the way too often multigenerational pattern of child abuse.

Our children are precious gifts, and they are our future. They deserve support and the resources to help them as they begin to travel on the path of life's incredible journey like the hatchling loggerhead turtles. I want the children we serve at Children's Advocacy Centers who have experienced abuse, traumas, and been victimized to believe that these childhood experiences do not stand in the way of all of their hopes and dreams and the endless opportunities that the future holds for them.

Terri Liles is the executive director of Helen's Haven Children's Advocacy Center in Hinesville, Georgia.

CHAPTER 15

Fly Baby, Fly

OUR window is always open. You have come to our nest with a broken wing and we take you into our fold. Mending broken wings is our business, and each and every broken wing is fixable. From time to time, each of us has an injured wing that is in need of some repair to make it stronger than before. This time, it just happens to be your wing that needs the work done to make sure YOU are healthier and safer than before.

You see, we've been at this fixing kids business a long time, and we will handle your broken wing ever so gently and with loving care, not waiting for the dust to settle. We will go to work right away on making things right with you. We'll start by opening our hearts and listening ears as you share your story behind what or who caused your broken wing. Your injury may be physical. It may come in the form of anger or sadness caused by either someone that you really trusted and once loved or may still love, or by someone that you never even liked in the first place. It could be a parent, friend, grandparent, brother or sister, cousin, someone you may just kind of, sort of know, or, in some cases, a total stranger that caused your pain.

As you share your story in our "safe" place, we'll be reminded of the many children who have walked through our doors day in and day out and who, over the years and one by one, chose to tell

"As we look to the sky, we'll be cheering 'Fly Baby, Fly!' And always, always know that if you ever lose even just one of those tools from your kit or need another dose of encouragement, we'll have our light on and the window open."

their story in a safe and happy place surrounded by people whose business it is to protect and love children. YOU HAVE BECOME THE MOST IMPORTANT PERSON TO US when you fly through our window. While you're here with us telling your story, you may even find your head spinning when you realize that someone believes your story, understands that what has happened is not your fault, and most of all, believes in YOU.

We will become your fiercest protector and the healer of your broken wing while holding your broken wing ever so gently so as not to make the injury worse. We'll teach you to first hum the words to the song "Fly Baby, Fly." If your injury needs medical attention, we will take care of that first in the same happy place where you came to tell your story. After we know that everything is okay with YOUR body, then it's time to do what needs to be done to make you a happy child no longer living in pain or fear. We do that by making sure that you have a safe person to talk with once you leave here, someone outside of your family who you can trust with all of your heart and one who will listen and teach you the skills to work through those bad memories so that one day soon, you will be the healthy and happy kid that you deserve to be, all the while having learned the words to "Fly Baby, Fly." That same person will be the one who gives you a very special tool kit to carry on your back as you fly again on your own. That kit will have all kinds of neat tools inside that will help you along the way when you have thoughts or feelings about the bad things that caused that broken wing in the first place. There will also be tools in there to help you in keeping yourself safe and ones that will help you throughout your life.

There have been so many kids just like you who were once hurt or injured just as you but who have placed their trust in us to fix their broken wings. One by one, we watched over those other kids while teaching them to sing "Fly Baby, Fly" and we'll do the same for you, while becoming your biggest cheerleader. We stay by each and every side until repairs are completed and until every wing is healthy and strong enough to hold you as you soar through the sky singing "Fly Baby, Fly." For some kids that have come and gone, it only took one season to repair the wing, but for others, they stayed with us through each and every season—winter, spring, summer, and fall. Then, one by one, that day came for each and every one to fly the coop. We've watched with love and joy as each soared through the skies as never before, and we'll do the same when it's your turn. We'll be at your side just as we have been at the sides of the many, many hurting children that have walked through our doors. But when you fly out of here just as the others have on their own time, the birds will be singing "Fly Baby, Fly" in harmony as we celebrate YOU.

You see, every wing is important in this life—from its color to its size, no two broken wings look alike. One day, when your wing has been put back together again and is strong enough to hold you as you soar through the skies on your own, it may look a little, or a lot, differently than before. Putting the wing back together again and giving it the support and time needed to heal is the part that we do, but we leave the finishing touches up to you like painting your feathered wing to wash away those bad memories. When you're ready and on your own time, you will fly the coop with that toolkit from us strapped to your back. That once broken wing will be new again and will forever be uniquely yours as you fly off with a heart of gold that can conquer the skies—with a beautiful new wing to make your set of wings perfectly complete, a set of wings that will take you to your happy place to do those great things that we always knew and believed that you could and would do. As we look to the sky, we'll be cheering "Fly Baby, Fly!" And always, always know that if you ever lose even just one of those tools from your kit or need another dose of encouragement, we'll have our light on and the window open.

Kim Adams is the executive director of the Children's Advocacy Center of Troup County in LaGrange, Georgia.

CHAPTER 16

The Hero is You

You are remarkable. You are special. You are significant. This is your journey, and we at the Children's Advocacy Center are here to help.

When you talked to the person who interviewed you at the CAC, you were the most important person in the room. This was the first step, and although it was a big step, we understand it may not have been easy.

And you are the most important person when you talk with your counselor at the Children's Advocacy Center.

At the Children's Advocacy Center, everybody is welcome. It does not matter the color of your skin, the language you speak, what you believe in, or who you love. Some kids who come here may feel they don't fit in, but here you are accepted for exactly who you are. We believe that everyone is extraordinary, and we hope you believe that too.

There was a TV show a long time ago called *Mr. Roger's Neighborhood*. Fred Rogers was the host of the show, and he taught kids lots of stuff. He said a very interesting thing about when people need help. Mr. Roger's said, "When I was a boy and I would see scary things in the news, my mother would say to me, 'Look for the helpers. You will always find people who are helping.' To this day, especially in times of "disaster," I remember my mother's words and I am always comforted by realizing that there are still so many helpers—so many caring people in this world."

The Children's Advocacy Center is full of helpers who care about you and see how special you are. Some of the helpers you will see every time you come to the center. But there are some helpers that you may never meet. Some of the helpers you will never meet are those people who work very hard to make sure all kids who need help have a Children's Advocacy Center to welcome them. All helpers at the Children's Advocacy Center believe that kids have very important feelings about the things that happen in their lives, and the counselors help kids talk about their feelings.

Do you know what feelings are? We have a lot of different feelings when something happens to us, around us, or when we see something or hear something. When kids come to the Children's Advocacy Center, they have a lot of different feelings about coming here. Happy, sad, angry, overwhelmed, scared, or surprise... Maybe you had some of these feelings when you came to the CAC. One reason we have feelings is to help us to survive and cope with the scary things that have happened and to be aware of when we are in danger. Quite often we talk about FEELINGS here at the center. Talking about feelings, even upsetting ones, helps kids feel better.

The helpers at the Children's Advocacy Center want you to know that all feelings are okay and everyone shows them differently. Sometimes feelings can be confusing and complicated. It is okay to be confused about what you are feeling. Don't worry, at the Children's Advocacy Center your helper will find many different ways that will help you feel comfortable and safe to talk about your feelings.

When you first came to the Children's Advocacy Center, you probably had a lot of feelings, some of them might have been the feeling of being scared, confused, or worried. Some children are scared they will not be believed. While other children are confused about why they need to talk to someone and answer so many questions. Many children are worried about what will happen next. Walking in the room and sitting down in the chair to talk about the bad, scary things that happened to you is so very brave. At the CAC, we want you to always remember that you are courageous, and you are strong.

It is not always easy to talk about what happened or to talk about our feelings. Sometimes it is hard to communicate how we are feeling even when we want to. When communication happens, understanding begins. We encourage you to communicate in lots of ways. You can use words, draw pictures, write poems, use puppets, or play games. There are many ways to communicate with or without using words.

We know some things may be harder to talk about than others. Giving your best is always good enough at a Children's Advocacy Center. If you do that, it is going to be worth it. You can do it, and you are not alone! When you came to the Children's Advocacy Center, you might have been the only child there, but did you know a lot of children go there every day? You may have even seen some of those children in your class or at the playground or in the grocery store. You cannot tell by looking at someone that something bad has happened to them. Just like no one can tell what happened to you by just looking at you. It is your choice to tell people or not to tell about the bad, scary thing that happened. You cannot change what happened, but you can change what happens next. We are here to help.

> *"No one should tell you how to feel about what happened. All feelings are okay. If you feel like crying, cry. If you feel like laughing, laugh. If you feel like smiling, smile. What if you feel angry? Some kids think that anger is not okay. But, there are a lot of healthy ways to show anger. For example, yell in a pillow, stomp the ground, or run around outside. At the Children's Advocacy Center, you and your helper will find safe and helpful ways to handle anger."*

What if you don't feel happy or motivated today? What if you feel down and cannot see the positive in yourself or in your day? Talk with your counselor or an adult you trust. Remember that everyone has those days, so it is okay.

We have just talked a lot about feelings. There are times when you can be tired of people asking you about how you feel. It is normal to feel that way, and it is all right to say that you do not want to talk about it. You can say, "Please do not ask me that. Just be with me. I will let you know when I want to talk about my feelings. I know you are trying to help." No one should tell you how to feel about what happened. All feelings are okay. If you feel like crying, cry. If you feel like laughing, laugh. If you feel like smiling, smile. What if you feel angry? Some kids think that anger is not okay. But, there are a lot of healthy ways to show anger. For example, yell in a pillow, stomp the ground, or run around outside. At the Children's Advocacy Center, you and your helper will find safe and helpful ways to handle anger.

Learning to be aware of your feelings in each moment—right here and now—will help you worry less about what happened or what might happen next. You can notice your feelings as they are happening by using your five senses: seeing, hearing, feeling, tasting, and smelling. Go outside and feel the sun shining on your face. Look around you and name everything you see. Listen to your favorite song and notice the words, rhythm, and melody. Be curious and find something new in the music you didn't notice before. Eat something new and pay attention to the taste and texture. Chew slowly and enjoy it. The next time you see a flower close your eyes and take a slow deep breath to enjoy the smell. Find a quiet, comfortable place in your house and sit still for a moment and notice everything around you. When you are doing this, try not to think about other things going on in your life; just be aware of the present moment—what is happening right now. You may get distracted with other thoughts, and that is all right. When those thoughts come, just let them go and bring your attention back to the things going on around you. With plenty of practice you will get better at noticing what is going on inside of you and around you. It will be easier to pay attention to the here and now instead of things that have already happened or might happen next.

Some of the things that have happened to you are tough, and some of the things we talk about at a Children's Advocacy Center can be tough too. It is to forget about the things in life that make us laugh and bring us joy. When we have these negative feelings at the Children's Advocacy Center one of our favorite things to do is to look at our coping collage. Everyone can have a coping collage, and everyone's collage will look different. To make your own coping collage all you need to do is think of some of your favorite things in your life, some things that make you smile or even make you laugh. Then you can take pictures of those things, cut out magazine pictures, print pictures online, or paint and draw your own pictures. These pictures are some things you can look at when you are feeling sad, scared, or angry.

You can always come back to look at those pictures when you need to smile. Remember a time when something happened that made you laugh? How does it make you feel remembering that now? Sometimes it seems like the bad, scary memories are bigger and louder than the good, happy ones. But all memories are important, and good memories help us feel better when we remember the bad, scary things. You see, your story is made up of all memories; the good and bad ones you have now and memories that will be made in your future.

At the Children's Advocacy Center, you have a strong, powerful voice, and you choose how to tell your own story. Some kids might feel nervous and some might feel excited about telling their stories. But remember, at the Children's Advocacy Center, you and your helper will work together, and you will not be alone.

Your story began before the bad, scary things happened and did not end when you told. It is normal for kids to worry or feel scared about what might happen after telling. But your story isn't over. Things that happened in your past did not change who you are. You are still the same cool, awesome kid you were before the bad, scary things happened. You were brave enough to talk about the bad, scary things, and we at the Children's Advocacy Center know you are brave enough to handle whatever happens next.

Can you think of someone who is brave enough to be called a hero? We, at the Children's Advocacy Center, think a lot of people are heroes. The heroes we think of are not in movies or comic books, and they don't wear capes or masks. The heroes at Children Advocacy Center are children just like you. Telling someone about the bad, scary things that happened is one of the bravest things a kid can do. When you look up the word "hero" in the dictionary, it says, "Hero—a person who is admired for great or brave

acts." At the Children's Advocacy Center, we say the HERO is YOU!
Thank you for being a HERO.

I am a HERO with voice loud and strong.
Not okay touching is always wrong.
My body is mine and no means halt.
Those who hurt kids are always at fault.
I may seem small but have no doubt
I told, I'm brave, I roar with a SHOUT!

*Dan Hillman is the executive director and Kari Viola is the Children's Advocacy
Center director at Child Enrichment: The Child Advocacy Center and Court
Appointed Special Advocates in Augusta, Georgia.*

CHAPTER 17

Overcoming

Introduction

THE BEAUTIFUL BRIDE
She was a beautiful bride. Following a successful four years of college and a year of study abroad, she was now committing to marriage with the love of her life. For more than fifteen years, we had watched her grow to become a lovely, confident, young woman. Marriage was the next chapter in her life and she chose a vineyard near the city for the ceremony. While the future might be challenging, it would, hopefully, not be as destructive as the first chapter when she was sexually abused.

THE STRONG ONE
The strong one we had called him. He was in middle school when we first met him and he had been strong even then—strong enough to tell his mom what the abuser did to him, strong enough to face the teasing and bullying from classmates, strong enough to testify against him. He took the support, the counseling, and the advocacy on his behalf and it left him even stronger.

SISTERS
Gang rape by twelve-year-old classmates was terrorizing and horrifying for the young victim. She spent months trying to cope with the physical and emotional wounds. An older sister became her best friend and comforter during the aftermath of the attack. The sibling suffered her own victimization for her failure at not being able to protect the twelve-year-old. The CAC counselor helped both girls. Because of this counseling

relationship, the young victim decided to talk to other girls whose pain was similar. She was passionate. She wanted each to have a counselor like her own at the CAC. She wanted each girl to recover from rape.

THE VALEDICTORIAN

Everyone was busy as checks were made on the language line that would be used to communicate with the immigrant mom coming for a 9:30 a.m. appointment at the children's advocacy center. The child would speak English while his mom would speak her native language. The appointment took over two hours of explanations from the language line. Earlier, mom and her son were removed to a shelter to protect the child from the perpetrator. Mom would lose her home, her job, and perhaps her precious son if she could not keep him safe. There were choices to be made.

THE BEAUTIFUL BRIDE

The bride's first chapter had come when she, at a very young age, began sexually acting out. While not always a cause for alarm, the interview and subsequent investigation revealed a case of sexual abuse by the stepfather. The mother, a professional who struggled to manage her job and a family of six, now had the most difficult task ahead. She needed help to restore her daughter's lost childhood while she faced her personal struggles with divorce, his confession, and now her financial hardship.

With a focus on healing and recovery, the mom and daughter regularly attended counseling at the children's advocacy center. There, hours turned into years of work and trials. Throughout the years they struggled with the child's behavior changes and the child's love for the perpetrator. They endured heartache together.

The trauma-focused, cognitive behavior therapy of the children's advocacy center was invaluable. The child was introduced to the arts and puppetry and her sessions became more successful. She expressed her feelings in her artwork to all who would notice. As she grew older, puppetry became an outlet and she presented programs for younger children throughout the community.

This case illustrates the truth that when you help the mom, the child responds positively. Commitment reigned. Mom was diligent and communicative. She faithfully saw that appointments were kept and she completed all assignments that were outside of her sessions. The work was difficult and intrusive. She was on an emotional roller-coaster caused by circumstances not of her making. By the time she reached the point of completing a trauma narrative, she was in control of her emotions and awed by the progress they were making.

Life went on. Mother and daughter shared their commitment to survive the ordeal, and with the help of many, they were successful.

THE STRONG ONE
The strong one's abuser had it all: comfortable income, plenty of free meals, and a reputation for being good, moral, and trusted. Unfortunately, he strayed to the darker side of humanity. He would sexually victimize vulnerable youth.

This middle school boy was brought to the children's advocacy center for victim support and counseling. He was strong. He had a supportive family who believed his story. As can sometimes unfortunately happen, news of these events were learned by some in the community. Adults were horrified at the violation, and children teased and bullied the young victim at school. Professionals were determined that justice would prevail. This pedophile would be convicted and sentenced for more years than he would live.

Pedophiles are often con artists. Sometimes they are highly regarded in the community. They are often believable, are generous, and may be found treating children to pizza or offering a ride so that they can be alone with the victim. Pedophiles will groom the victim with small gestures that grow into more serious violations with time and frequency. On average, pedophiles will molest a large number of children and they will continue to molest until they are caught.

In this case, the family would offer strength and the middle school boy did not waiver when he had to face his molester in court. Counseling had helped him cope with the experience and advocacy prepared him for his day in court. Following court and sentencing, he continued his education and completed counseling, knowing that his perpetrator would never victimize another child.

This client, the strong one, did not try to escape from the words "child sexual abuse victim." He overcame his molestation, is employed, and remains strong today.

SISTERS
She was in middle school and meeting a group of classmates to work on a science project. It was after leaving her school for the long walk to the farm that the sexual assault took place. Three boys gang raped the eleven-year-old. There was no one to call out to or tell when she arrived at the country house where she lived with her mom and older sister.

She had initially seen one counselor but had no further interest in talking to anyone. It was months later before the school counselor referred her to the children's advocacy center within the county. She was troubled and cautious when she came to counseling. Her sister had become her confidant and closest friend since the incident.

This new counselor could relate to the eleven-year-old. She required her to stay on task and work at retelling of her victimization. The counselor was firm but understood the frailty of the young victim who had been to some dark places. Together they made progress. The victim began to write in her journal. She began to heal and her desire to help others prevailed. The young victim reached out to other victims and encouraged them all to go to counseling so they could begin to heal as she had.

THE VALEDICTORIAN
The child protection services investigator had called the children's advocacy center for an appointment for a forensic interview and forensic medical examination. Law enforcement made a commitment to be present for both and they all traveled from a neighboring county within the judicial circuit to the children's advocacy center.

The family advocate made certain the language line was available because no one was available to speak Mom's native language in the rural county. Mom spoke no English. The son was fluent in English and the top student in his class. He was able to help as the multidisciplinary team worked to discuss the case. Present other than the mom and her son were the medical director, forensic interviewer, victim advocate, law enforcement detective, and child protective services investigator. The counselor completed the team.

The multidisciplinary team was at work. During the forensic interview the child disclosed some inappropriate sexual behavior on the part of Mom's boyfriend in the household. During the medical examination, the family nurse practitioner reassured him that his body was okay. He was anxious that the perpetrator had harmed his body and this reassurance began the process of emotional healing for the child.

The child protection investigator had contacted the local shelter who would be able to accommodate Mom and her child. They were able to get some of their things as they moved out of their home.

It does take a village to help those affected by child sexual abuse. Both Mom and son were provided counseling although Mom would be limited by her language barrier. The language line would be of use again in counseling sessions, although the child would be instrumental in helping the mom understand the rapidly changing climate caused by child sexual abuse. There were choices to be made. Hopefully, Mom will make good choices and counseling will strengthen both her and her son.

CONCLUSION

Child sexual abuse is a crime. It is a heinous crime against children because it often involves someone they know and love. The numbers are staggering when one out of four girls and one out of six boys may be sexually abused by their eighteenth birthday. Child sexual abuse is an epidemic.

Many children, nine out of ten in fact, never tell. The stories here, while fictitious, are illustrative of accounts of children who receive services from a children's advocacy center. Not all of the children who come to the center disclose abuse. Not all of the children have supportive family who believe them when they do disclose. The good news from the children advocacy centers is that trained staff members know to say "I believe you" and provide encouragement, support, and resources. The multidisciplinary team is vital to the success of the child's case and the judicial process plays an important role.

Regardless of the outcome, the most important factor is that the child is safe and can begin to heal through the many services provided to the family including the forensic interview, the forensic medical exam, specialized counseling, and victim advocacy. An abused child deserves the intense care, support, and resources that a children's advocacy center provides.

If you are beginning a journey with an allegedly abused child there are two things to remember: (1) you will not go through this alone, and (2) there is hope and there is healing even in the darkness of child sexual abuse.

Carol Donaldson is the executive director of the Sunshine House Children's Advocacy Center in Swainsboro, Georgia.

CHAPTER 18

Looking Glass Letters of Hope and Healing

Dear Child,

Set your sights high. My dream is that through everything you have experienced you will become a strong, brave, and successful woman. I hope that you will grow up and see that you can make something of this life. It is unfair what you have been through. Although it seems as though your family has been ripped apart, your mother is by your side and so is your family at Harmony House.

Not only did someone take away your innocence, they took away your brother. I know you understand that he needs help from the abuse that he suffered, but when you are eight it is hard to understand why you can't visit your older brother who you looked up to. I know that you miss him because you have told me this much. I hope that you both can grow up and reform a healthy relationship, but it is possible that along with your childhood this man has taken your brother as well. So for now, stay strong and believe in yourself.

We know that children are resilient; we know that there is hope for you. Since the abuse your life has not been much easier. Your father is now away because of his

> "I like to think that by putting these words onto paper it brings them to life. Although every child may never read these words I find comfort in knowing they are out there. I am convinced that when we say something positive toward a person, it follows their spirit."

struggle with substance abuse. I hope that instead of following the family pattern you overcome and discover there are healthy ways to cope that do not include self-medication.

I hope that you find comfort in the fact that your abuser is locked away. I hope that you feel safe in your home. I trust that as you get older you feel that justice was brought to you and your family. When you testified against your abuser, you stood tall and did not flinch. I know that strength is inside you and I foresee that when things are hard you will be able to reach in and find that strength and you will persevere.

I don't know what is in store for your future, but I know it can include greatness. On the days that I met you, you wanted to be so many wonderful professions, like a detective, a teacher, and one time, me. I want to have inspired you to continue your education, and maybe one day go to college and make those dreams come true. Your story has stuck with me over the past few years and guided me to continue trying to make a difference in our community. One day, I see childhood sexual abuse to be something of the past, but until that day we will continue working to save little girls and boys like you and your brother from situations that are not fair.

I like to think that by putting these words onto paper it brings them to life. Although every child may never read these words I find comfort in knowing they are out there. I am convinced that when we say something positive toward a person, it follows their spirit. I wrote these letters originally, because I thought it would be a great way to reflect on the cases and the emotions that accompany working with families. However, in doing this letter for this chapter I am inspired. I thought, "What if we could really send these, how great would that be for our families?" I think that receiving a letter could help victims move down their road to recovery. If we could write letters for all of our families, not only would it be good for them, but it would also be a form of positive self-care for the team.

The first letter was from the advocate's point of view to a child. This second letter is a little different in that it is written to adults who were child victims. I hope these letters help victims to see that it is possible to move forward and lead a satisfying life after their traumatic experience.

Dear Survivor,

As an adult survivor of childhood sexual abuse, your journey has become a story that motivates and inspires others to overcome the trauma and beat the odds. Not only are you an inspiration to those who find themselves in similar situations, you are an inspiration to me and the amazing team of people who have known you for many years. There have been moments where I have felt let down and beat up by the system, but I remember your strength, I remember how brave you were all those years ago, and I remember why I stay devoted to my job.

You were barely sixteen years old; you had been in too many foster homes since the age of twelve, and once again we would find out that the system was not working in your favor. On the morning you first disclosed your abuse, the social services caseworker saw you arrive at the court hearing for yet another placement review and she knew something was terribly wrong. You were and still are a beautiful young woman; you always took great pride in your appearance, and like many teenage girls your age you were always groomed meticulously. However, on this day, something was different, you had experienced a life-changing trauma and it had already shattered you beyond imagination. I am proud to say that we were able to finally surround you with a team that would offer support and that you would finally get the help from the system that you deserved. Although we were able to give you a team, we did not teach you how to be brave, and we did not teach you to have aspirations in life that was already grounded within your personality.

Looking back on this day many years ago, I remember that I had just stepped in the forensic interview room for one of the first times since my recent training. I was so nervous and afraid that my failures and inexperience as an interviewer would let you down once again. It was a responsibility that just seemed too overwhelming, but there you were—no turning back now.

We were both clearly frustrated and scared. Not only had you been neglected by the system, you were now in your worst-case scenario because of the system and now having to talk with a perfect stranger. You had been harmed early that morning and you were unsure about how the system would or could help. Then you were willing to give a complete stranger your narrative of something so very horrible with the hope that you could stop this from happening to another person. Our interview was one of a kind . . . you took control! I know you could tell I was nervous, but you were calming. At that moment I knew you would make it . . . **you** would survive. And survive you have indeed. What a beautiful self-confident person you have become. You wanted a better life for your kids than what was dealt to you, and even after all of the hardships in your life you were able to become successful and give that dream life to your own family.

Many times you have struggled with feelings of guilt, shame, or blame like many survivors do, but you were able to work through these common natural responses by reaching out to those who could and will always be there to help. Many times you have re-embraced counseling and sought other ways to keep healing and surviving. You are able to have healthy adult relationships, which can be hard for some childhood sexual abuse victims because you have eagerly sought the tools and resources necessary. You gained the coping skills so important to "moving on," by having the strength to seek help. The percentage of girls who experience a sexual assault in their life is shockingly high, but our hope is that number begins to decrease as social norms and acceptance of that behavior cease to exist. A percentage of those girls will never have access to services necessary in developing coping skills. The number of women who experience psychiatric disorders is higher than those who have experienced childhood sexual abuse. Some of the common psychiatric disorders linked to childhood sexual abuse include substance abuse, Post Traumatic Stress Disorder (PTSD), and depression. Had the Child Advocacy Center and your Social Services caseworker not been in place, my fear is that these disorders would have become your fate. Your acceptance of the help and honesty about your situation allowed you to overcome the odds and live a healthy adult lifestyle.

Your life has come full circle. You are able to live out your dreams with your own family as well as provide support for your family.

For the future, I look forward to seeing you survivors and looking at the ways you all overcome your past and create a beautiful life for yourselves. I wish that I could say the future holds no victims and therefore no survivors, but today that is not the case. However, your futures are much brighter, thanks to the people who are there to help you through recovery. I see healthy relationships and successful careers. I see parents and family members who are happy and have let go of any weight following them from their abusers. I see people who feel confident and justified and ready to take on the world. You all bring a type of strength that is hard for anyone to understand. Your bravery will show through your successes and later your legacies. I look forward to seeing all that you accomplish.

Laurie Whitworth is the executive director and Adreinne Bass is the Director of Client Services at the Harmony House Children's Advocacy Center in Royston, Georgia.

CHAPTER 19

You are Having a Normal Reaction
to an Abnormal Situation

You are having a normal reaction to an abnormal situation.

Child abuse should not happen. We as a society do not bring life on to this earth for this life to be abused and traumatized as a child. However, this happens to children. And it happens often. Moving through the pain and emotions after a child has been hurt is hard. It may be one of the most difficult times you encounter. The emotions you feel during this time may fluctuate greatly and be confusing. That is why you must know that you are having a normal reaction to an abnormal situation. There is no right or wrong way to feel after finding that a child you love has been abused. But there are a few standard stages of grief that most caregivers of children that have been hurt may go through over time. Here are some of those stages explained by someone who has seen caregivers go through these stages over and over again.

Denial is commonly the first emotion I have seen caregivers experience after first learning a child they love has been abused. This denial may come in the form of not believing the child's story for a small moment of time to for the rest of their lifetime. This denial is a coping mechanism from their brain because at that moment

> *"Self-care is a practice; a daily practice to take care of ourselves. As caregivers, we give care to others; these others we love dearly. For us to truly take good care of them, we must take care of ourselves first."*

it is too hard to believe that their child has been a victim of abuse. I've seen this denial present itself in caregivers not believing that they heard correctly the child's statement about being abused. They may feel that the authorities involved may not be telling the truth when they are told about the abuse. They may attempt to add up dates and times the child spent alone with the abuser and feel that there wasn't enough opportunity for the abuse to occur. They may feel the child is confused about a situation that wasn't actually abuse. However, it manifests itself; denial is usually short lived and then the caregiver must come to terms with the fact that a child they love has been hurt. It is difficult to manage the emotions ahead.

Caregivers have told me when they first heard the news of their child's abuse they were in shock, like the room became physically smaller. Some told me they had a hard time hearing for a while. They felt words were echoing in their heads. Some felt an extreme heat in their body and began to sweat while others felt extreme cold and their teeth began to chatter. Some felt very nauseous and some even became physically ill. Caregivers have told me they felt numb to their surroundings, like they are watching the others in the room. Not able to hear what is told to them. Not able to express themselves. When recalling when they were told, they don't remember the exact events of how. Some caregivers become very upset and cry. Some become very upset and show rage. These are common symptoms of the shock of learning that a child you love has been hurt.

Bargaining is the next step in the stages after learning that a child you love has been a victim of abuse. The bargaining is another usually short stage, just as denial. This bargaining is usually expressed through thoughts of "what if." Such as, what if I hadn't trusted that person to watch after my child, this would not have happened. Or what if I hadn't gone to work that day, I wouldn't have left my child with that person. Or what if I had never enrolled my child in that program, they would have not been around that person. The "what ifs" can go on and on. This is a way that the caregiver is trying to take back some control in the situation. They are trying to put the blame on them or some other person than the abuser to gain this control. We can "what if" almost every life event, but it still doesn't change what happened. It is a coping mechanism to find control in the past. To find control in the future, there must be a cause that the caregiver could control as to why this happened to their child.

I think the "what ifs" lead to the beginning of the extreme guilt that all the caregivers I have worked with feel once they learn that their child has been a victim of abuse. Caregivers commonly feel guilt for almost anything negative that happens to their children, even if they are at fault or not. That is part of being a caregiver, not a healthy reaction, but a common reaction. We as humans try to create an image of perfection, an image we can never live up to. This image is not real. We are never going to be perfect enough for this image of perfection we have created for ourselves. Having a child that never experiences hurt is part of this image of perfection. When a child in our care has been hurt, we feel extreme guilt even if the hurt is from no fault of our own. It is not helpful to dwell in this guilt. Put the blame where it belongs, on the abuser. Work toward what you do actually have control over. That is the healing of you and your child.

The next two stages intertwine with each other. It is common for caregivers to move through these stages together, experiencing one more than the other at times. But they certainly feed off of each other. These stages last the longest of all the stages thus far after learning that a child you love has been abused. These two stages are anger and depression.

I had the wonderful opportunity to work with caregivers of children who had been sexually abused within a support group for many years. Some members of this group attended these group sessions on a regular basis for years. I was able to support them as they moved back and forth from depression to anger.

The depression shows itself in physical ways. Caregivers may eat too much or eat too little. They don't enjoy activities or people the way they used to. They have trouble concentrating on almost anything. They may not be able to stop thinking about what happened to their child. It is a noticeable difference to anyone who truly knows them. It affects their relationships at work, school, and at home. It effects how they feel about themselves and everyone around them. There seems to be a gloom over their spirit.

The joined emotional stage is anger. This rage can flare up at the abuser, which is justified, but may result in negative consequences if a caregiver acts out on this anger to the abuser. Unfortunately, the law still protects a person from being abused, even if the abuse is a reaction from someone that person abused. Caregivers may have uncontainable rage at everyday life situations. They may be seen to have a "short fuse" whereas they didn't before learning that their child has been a victim of abuse. They may lash out at strangers, those they love, those they have to be in contact with because of work or school, etc. Unfortunately, the anger doesn't help them feel any better either. Especially when expressed in negative ways to others. They may then feel guilty for acting out of control when expressing their anger.

This then feeds right back into the depression. Depression and anger flow back and forth through the caregiver for long periods of time. It may last for years, it may never go away; that is unless the caregiver takes control over their own well-being and seeks help. If they look, they will find a way to coming to terms with the anger and depression due to learning that a child they love has been abused.

This leads us to the final stage, acceptance. Acceptance doesn't mean that the abuse was okay. It doesn't mean that everything is wonderful. It doesn't mean that the caregiver, their child, or their family is back to the way it was before the abuse. That will never happen. Acceptance means that the caregiver accepts that the abuse happened, that they are learning each day to live with it, they are learning ways to take care of themselves and the child that was abused to help them feel better. And feeling better will not happen every day. There will be days, weeks, or months that the anger and the depression come back. But by this stage, the caregiver has found support and resources to help them work through the anger and the depression and to help their child work through their own emotions about the abuse. There will be good days, there will be wonderful days just like there will be days of pain. Having supports in place to help the caregiver work through those days of pain will help them understand and find acceptance into what happened to their child.

I cannot speak about the stages most caregivers experience when learning that a child they love has been abused without speaking about self-care. Self-care is the most important thing we can practice not only for ourselves but also for those around us. Life gives us stress. Stress builds up over time. We must practice self-care to break down that buildup of stress, because that build up will seep into our lives and act out in ways that we do not like. It makes us stressed out humans, hard to be around. We act out because of the stress we are holding on to. Self-care is a practice; a daily practice to take care of ourselves. As caregivers, we give care to others; these others we love dearly. For us to truly take good care of them, we must take care of ourselves first.

It takes thought and time to practice self-care. First, you must identify a few things that you can do for yourself to take care of yourself. It's not that difficult if you think about it. What do you enjoy to do? What can you do that takes away stress rather than causes stress? The answer to this question is different for everyone. It may be a hot, long bath. It may be watching something funny on TV. It may be walking outside with your dog. It may be talking to your best friend. It may be meditation or praying. Whatever it may be, we need a few of these self-care tactics to keep in our tool box when we are feeling stressed. It is a healthy practice to do these self-care techniques even before we begin to feel the stress. Doing them daily is the key; doing them as often as possible.

That brings me to the next piece of self-care: finding the time. We make time in our day for lots of things that are not self-care. If we begin to place self-care as important as the many other things that we do in our day that are not self-care, then we will find the time to take care of ourselves. It doesn't have to be a great deal of time. But when you know that you are important enough, that you take the time to take care of yourself, your body, mind, and soul will thank you through clearer thoughts, better rest and disposition in life.

One more thing, a piece of self-care for caregivers that have learned that a child they love has been abused is allowing themselves to feel the emotions. It is allowing themselves to process what it is that they are feeling. This may be painful. Some caregivers do a great job at keeping themselves very busy so they don't have to feel the pain. The pain doesn't care. It will find a way to sneak into their life and disrupt it. Why give the pain that power over your life? Take that control back and let yourself feel. I recommend you allowing fifteen to thirty minutes to be alone and think about the pain. Think purposefully about the horrible stuff that keeps popping up in your thoughts. It only has to be fifteen to thirty minutes. Set a timer; when the time is up go back to being busy. You will find that once your mind knows that it has time set aside to process these painful thoughts, then that is when it will be processed. These thoughts won't flood your day and make you feel out of control. They have a place to be thought of, you decided that place, and you control these painful thoughts. They may lessen with time or become very strong at times. You may find peace in knowing that there is a time you have set aside to process these painful thoughts. Be good to yourself, practice self-care. The thing about self-care is only you can do it for yourself.

Sally Sheppard is the executive director of The Cottage Sexual Assault Center and Children's Advocacy Center in Athens, Georgia.

CHAPTER 20

Thought, Word, and Deed

THOUGHT. From you, the caregiver's perspective

Your mind can't fathom what the detective from the county Sheriff's Department just explained to you. Then in the humble place of your mind you realize now in looking back that some things make sense. Life has never been that easy, but you thought you had things under control. Your vision tunnels down to a pinpoint of light. The questions flood over you. Who can help me? Who do I trust and who will help me protect my child? Who will judge me? Why does this remind me of fears and shortcomings within myself? How do I move through this legal system? Will my child be brave enough and feel safe enough to talk about horrible secrets that have happened to him or her? What steps and attitudes do I need to help my child now, and what can I expect regarding their needs as they grow?

WORD. A few from an advocate's perspective

It has been my great honor to work with juveniles and their parents in a professional educational capacity. I am in awe of the challenges kids and their supportive caregivers experience today. For families with the additional trauma of current or past sexual abuse, many issues like trust, communication, safety, and support will arise again and again as children grow and hopefully evolve through their youth and into productive well-balanced adults. I have experienced and witnessed firsthand some of the choices that lead to less desired consequences. This includes walking up to an open coffin at the front of the church. Teen and young adults are starting to really understand the transition necessary to move to independence. It can be scary, and if you do not have a set of tools to help you along the way, it can and will get bumpy.

My experience has shown often times abused children become involved with law enforcement and the court system. As well, some statistics have shown that IQ scores of children who have been victimized can fall below the general average of 100.

This is simply demonstrated by a fourteen-year-old boy referred to the juvenile courts foundations program due to truancy, runaway, and unruly child issues. When asked what he did after school, his reply was "I sleep." One of many thoughts that went through my head was, "Well at least he is not getting into trouble." Upon further conversation I asked, "Do you read anything besides school assignments?" His reply was no. At the end of the class I assigned him to read and orally report back the next week at class at least the table of contents of a book I handed him. That next week being his last class session, a question asked to all youth completing the class is, "What is one thing you have learned from this class?" To my surprise and thankfulness, this awesome young man who took almost an awkward amount of time to reply but finally blurted out to even his surprise, "I got to get a hobby!" As he walked out with his certification of completion, he asked, "If that is your book and you don't want it any more, can I have it?"

You and supportive loved ones are critical to the youth in moving beyond just safety and permanency and into "well-being." State supreme courts, government agencies, and local advocacy groups are all moving into this understanding.

Well-being is understanding the impact of environment, personal relationships, and experiences in life. Sexual abuse survivor Kevin Mulcahey phrased it "the perfect storm." A child retains memories of learned fear and thus continues the trauma even after the elimination of the immediate danger.

Healthy development depends on the quality and reliability of a child's relationships with the important people in their lives, within and outside the family. A child's brain development depends on these relationships.

Heightened stress has been shown to impair the development of the brain that is vital for the execution of function such as making, following and altering plans, controlling and focusing attention, controlling impulsive behaviors as well as the ability to hold and incorporate new information in decision making.

Trauma sets off a survival alarm system that with continued trauma is too easily triggered and too slow to shut down. The child therefore is on constant hyperalert, overinterprets signs of danger, over-reacts to normal situations, and has difficulty with attachment and trust, particularly with authority figures. In 2015, Kevin Mulcahey spoke to the Children's Advocacy Centers of Georgia's Annual "One Team" Conference in Response to Child Abuse and Neglect about his personal experience of sexual abuse:

"The betrayal is greater than the abusive sex act," he said.

How youth form relationships with adults is important as they move from adolescence into young adulthood. If these relationships are developed on the basis of fear, shame, guilt, intimidation, and/or a general atmosphere of chaos, the negative results just seem to build upon one another.

Find in your area community resources that provide support to you that aid in the development of life skills that focus on secure relationship building, positive internal talk, emotional control, simple coping skills, and the understanding that constant observation and adjustment is needed to maintain personal and professional positive functional adult relationships. As the saying goes, "Life is not in finding yourself, life is about creating yourself."

All humans need two things to grow and thrive regardless of age.

- To feel *safe*, and
- To feel a sense of *unconditional* love and/or support.

Finding, understanding, and using the tools that build these feelings within yourself and then to those you care for can be overwhelming. Becoming a self-sufficient, cooperative, mature, and healthy community-minded adult in our culture of entitlement is an uphill climb. The idea of accountability, personal responsibility, and consequence of one's actions is difficult when viewed through the perspective of trauma.

It is necessary to develop tools for more effective family relationships. Some of these tools include:

- *Responding to adversity.* Out of hurt and anger many respond to adversity defensively, denying that they are responsible and shift blame to others. Responsibility needs to be seen as the duty of the individual to accept our own actions. This lessens the negative chain of reactions to come. Fear and anxiety are diminished as the individual integrates courage and strength to be truthful; the sense of being a victim diminishes as wisdom from these experiences are brought forth.

- *Moocher vs. Producer.* Instead of clamoring for entitlements and rights, there is the emphasis of finding and fulfilling your purpose. This is a perspective to move beyond the trauma of the past to the empowerment of your in-the-present goal setting and the awesome feeling that comes from achievement of follow through. The trophy in your life is self-esteem. This is critical to sound decision making.

- *A foundation for growth.* Regardless of outcome, to unconditionally support your child is the prepared ground required to plant seeds of relationship building and opens the mind to new and improved ways of decision making in the best interest of oneself and that of others. This support aids in the feeling of safety. When a human feels safe and loved, he is able to take chances. Try new things and ways of being. That is the evolution of things.

DEED. Putting into action the best interests of you and your teen

First of all, let it be said right up front, parenting or supporting teens and young adults is a big deal. A good friend of mine with much older children

smirked at me while I grumbled about my kids in their "terrible two's."
All she said was, "Just wait till they are teens!" Oh my, how right she was.

Young adults can make decisions that have dire consequences while their
brains do not mature until well into their mid-twenties. Humans in their
teens and early twenties who have experienced trauma function many
times from a base survival alarm of fight or flight. They function on
emotional extremes. Their difficulty to trust and their life experience
with authority makes it very difficult to develop a relationship. They are
distant and pompous. With developing self-awareness, teens struggle with
stress and anger. Without an adult influence that consistently has their
best interest, they will turn to peers. Their friends are their support.
These are humans who may know no more than they do. Remember our
society tells these young adults to take control, make decisions, grow up,
and be somebody. Their trauma-based life experience is much different.
These teens understand the darkness in this lifetime. Parents and support
providers have to move from there.

A very honest Mom in a panic situation with her daughter admitted out
loud through tears, "I know I have been such a bad example to her." I told
her that in her admission and accountability within the trauma unfolding
in this family's lives, that is a place to start. I was proud of the mom.

A journal entry of mine continues to give me hope:

Night shall pass into clear bright day.

Understand your weaknesses as ways to better yourself. Humility provides
the best teacher to ever come closer to the image of God that you are to
be with one another.

Before me today my failures are in my own hand.

With useless tears I give it up to thee so happily it may win some use, some
beauty yet.

As the saying goes: There's so much good in the worst of us, and so much bad in the best of us that it hardly behooves any of us to talk about the rest of us.

Start here, now, today. You can't change yesterday. Who knows what tomorrow will bring. You must live in the now. Empower yourself with the knowledge from the experience of trauma and how it has developed the darkness in your family.

You remain critical to them because young adults still search for a place to steady themselves. When they can't find it they panic. They react without thinking. It is so important for you to find times and places to form lasting relationships with teens in general and especially those who have trauma in their lives.

- *Take advantage of everyday times to talk.* Sometimes we forget to sit and eat a sandwich together and talk about interests and activities. Ask about friends. Acknowledge their point of view. Take as much time talking about the good qualities and behaviors as you do telling them your hopes and boundaries. Even if things turn to disagreement, know that is their way of forming their own identity. Keep your ideas, hopes, and expectations brief but don't stop reaching out. Be undeterred, they may get tired of you sticking your nose in and just open the door and let you in.

- *Respect one another.* Be the role model. Again, Kevin Mulcahey spoke at the conference and cautioned the room packed full of professionals, community members, and parents:

"There is no common or typical case to a victim."

Kevin Mulcahey reminded all of us: "This is not your story. It is the victim's. Don't show off."

Respect with young adults means knowing when to back off.

Relationship is cooperation. Too often today relationships connote ownership. With ownership comes expectancy of behavior. There is no ownership in a healthy relationship. This is important when seen through the lens of parenthood. You need to have a space around you which you operate without feeling obligated to someone else. At the same time you can't make demands on someone else without allowing them the same right. Working from this place every day will offer the opportunity to develop a relationship on a whole new level. Rules without a relationship will equal rebellion. Teens and young adults respond more to how you are regarding them than they do to our words and actions.

- *Thought on the use of energy.* Universal energy principles are that "like" energy attracts "like" energy. Energy is not judged as bad or good energy. Energy just is. Energy flows along through your field of attention and this energy is expressed through your habits, attitudes, deeds, and beliefs. Your best interest decisions—yours and your child's—come from the nonjudgmental examination of how your "attention energy" is being expressed within your life. Real wisdom only comes from life experiences well examined. Be consistent and clear about what you desire. Barbara Marciniak, author of *Bringers of the Dawn*, wrote, "That clarity will attract similar circumstances through which you may explore that desire. Mixed feelings will bring mixed outcomes." Besides consistency and clarity, my experience has shown that the energy of patience, humility, open-mindedness, and flexibility are energy principles that aid in the growth and evolution of positive human relationships.

Maya Angelo said, "When you know better you do better."

- *The Mind. Ask yourself.* "What mentality am I communicating out to another within each moment or situation during the day? Am I a creator, a maintainer, or a destroyer?" Ponder if what you are doing is working in the best interest first of yourself then to those you love.

- *The Body. Feel the emotional perspective.* Parents need to understand that with all the emerging demands for independence, worries about peer acceptance, pressures of school and extracurricular activities, and a continuous search for self-identity, kids are on a physical and emotional roller-coaster.

- ***Your Spirit. That next best version of yourself.*** Find your peace. You can't build relationships by dragging the person and process in kicking and screaming. Build relationships by remembering the good times, activities, and places. Listen and learn. Communicate with each other. Teach, and where appropriate and open-mindedness is present, correct. Do not coerce or control. Create a safe place to allow others to ponder their lives anew, whatever that means to them.

Michelle Edwards is the executive director of the Forsyth County Children's Advocacy Center in Cumming, Georgia.

CHAPTER 21

Not to Spoil the Ending for You, *but Everything is Going to be Okay!*

You have been brought to a child advocacy center because of something that has happened to you or because of something someone thinks happened to you. You may be scared, confused, or simply concerned. So what happens now? As the title says, everything is going to be okay.

It certainly does not feel like that right now. Don't expect it to! Life is forever changed for you and your family. What you need to know is that we hear you. Whatever you tell us, we hear you. Regardless of whether it leads to a conviction of the wrongdoer, we hear you. And isn't that wonderful? We hear you and are here for you. Don't forget, YOU are the brave one. You have taken a chance and told and we hear you.

I once met a young girl who I will never forget. She was the youngest of sisters and was the last to be abused. She didn't mean to tell, but when it came out, she was the brave one. She told us what had happened even though it was not easy. Her mother did not believe her, her sisters waivered in their belief and sometimes she was all by herself. But she had us and she

> *"If you do not hear anything else I've said in this chapter, please don't forget therapy. If you do, you'll be running this race for the rest of your life and it will be as if you are in a cage with a wheel like a gerbil runs on. You will run and run and never move forward, never get anywhere, spend lots of energy doing it and never be able to get out."*

had a father who believed her and did everything he could to protect her. And guess what, we listened when she told and we heard her. It took a long time to resolve and involved a lot of meetings with professionals, family members, lawyers, etc. Is it over? Yes and no. Yes, the trial is over yes, the perpetrator is behind bars; and yes, she is safe. But is it over in her mind? Most likely the answer is no. Her family doubted her and I'm sure that left some pain behind, maybe feelings of betrayal, doubt, or fear but there was also joy, love, and protection from other family and friends. She will learn to work through those feelings just like you will learn to work through all the feelings you have right now.

So let's get back to you. You are here to tell us about something that has happened to you or that someone close to you thinks happened. I hope you will hear this: disclosure, *the action of making new or secret information known*, is a process. Sometimes when a person tells us their secrets they tell us all the secrets they have about the incidents that have happened to them. However, most of the time, they do not. Most of the time, they tell us enough for whatever has been happening to stop but not all the details.

For example, a child may tell us that she was touched in the private areas two times and because of that disclosure the alleged perpetrator is taken out of the home. They may try to bury the rest or pretend that what they initially told is all that really happened. Given the opportunity, they may tell us more over time, such as the perpetrator actually touched her private with his private, making the allegations even more serious, or they may not. Sometimes children may tell us what happened and then take it back because they are afraid of the perpetrator or because the family has pressured them to change their story. It could also happen because the perpetrator has been forced to move out of the house and now mom can't pay the bills and the only way he can come back is for the child to say that they were lying or they made it all up. We both know that is probably far from the truth. Did you tell us the truth? I hope so. Did you tell it all? Chances are you didn't. For now, we have to accept that and recognize that is where you are in the process. But I hope you won't stop telling now that the incident is no longer happening to you. I hope that you will continue your healing and talk about all the things that happened to you.

My recommendation is that you get formal therapy. It is great to talk to friends, but you need to talk to someone trained in trauma-focused therapy. They have special skills to help you through the healing process. They work with others who have been through incidents similar to yours. It is important to find a person you are comfortable talking to. Make sure you talk to your parents about this. You don't have to tell them what you talk about, but you should talk to them about how comfortable you are with the therapist. Talking about trauma is hard work, so it is important you feel comfortable with your therapist.

Your therapist will help you learn to live with the trauma you have experienced. She/he will help you learn coping skills for the times when you re-experience the trauma of the incident. These moments in time are often referred to as triggers. And yes, there will be triggers—those moments in your future when a smell or sound or experience reminds you of the incident or the person who did this to you. Here's the bad news, you will experience the pain of the incident all over again. But the coping skills you learn from your therapist will help you understand that it was just an event that happened to you and it is not happening now; you are safe and you will move on. It will hurt, but through the years the hurt will impact you less and you will recover quicker. You will learn that this incident is only one event in your history of things that has happened to you. The incident does not have to define you—it happened to you, it is NOT you.

If you do not hear anything else I've said in this chapter, please don't forget therapy. If you do, you'll be running this race for the rest of your life and it will be as if you are in a cage with a wheel like a gerbil runs on. You will run and run and never move forward, never get anywhere, spend lots of energy doing it and never be able to get out. At some point you have to jump off that wheel and work your way out of the cage that abuse has trapped you in. Your therapist, with support of your family and friends, will help you do that. They will, through their actions, show you that you are important and worthy of their trust, respect, and love. Let them retrain you to respect yourself and love yourself so that you can grow to love others.

Some other words that I hope you hear is, you cannot make this go away. You can't pray it away, wish it away, or hope it away. It happened to you, not your mama, not your daddy, not your cousin—YOU. It happened and it is now part of your history, just like learning to walk, learning to ride a bike, or learning to drive. At each of those stages you progressed a little more becoming more independent. Not this stage, the abuse you suffered may cause you to retreat in your development. You may find yourself becoming more childlike, more dependent on others, needing to constantly be around other, or simply wanting to be alone. This may be confusing to you and concerning to your caregivers, but you will recover. Do not fret, you will be forever changed, but remember this is part of your history and only an incident that happened to you. It's not you.

Okay, you say you got that. What now? You have to learn what to do with all that information. What does it mean for you, for your family? First, you have to admit that it happened to you, and you've done that. GO, brave one! You have to accept that it was not your fault and it was not your responsibility. This may be harder because if it is like most situations, the person who hurt you tried really hard to make sure you felt you were somehow responsible for what happened or even worse, that somehow you wanted this to happen or you asked for it. You may think to yourself, "But I didn't say no." Chances are you didn't because you were scared of what would happen to you or someone or something you know and love if you did. Or maybe you would have lost something dear to you if you did or a multitude of other threats, bribes, or promises. Once you realize that these special privileges came at a high cost, that was you and your well-being, then you can begin to accept that you were not responsible for what happened. Then you can put the blame where it should be: on the person who hurt you. With that simple act begins the realization that this person whom you trusted hurt you and it was NOT your fault.

Okay, so it wasn't your fault, it was their fault. This leads to a whole other layer of concern, TRUST. If you trusted this person, as most likely you did, because that person relied on that fact to keep you quiet, then how do you ever trust again? I go back to therapy. This may be something that happens later in life or it may be something that you discuss in your initial therapy. Either way, learning to trust happens over time. You will not wake up one day and say, "Hey, today is the day I start trusting everyone again." That won't happen. It will be slow and arduous, kind of like the turtle that beat the hare in the race. Do you remember that story? So the hare (or rabbit) decides that he is going to challenge the turtle to a race. He knows it will be so easy to beat the turtle in the race that he runs about halfway through the course and decides to take a little nap while the whole time the turtle is slowly making his way to the finish line. The hare wakes up just in time to see the turtle about a yard from the finish line. Try as he might, the hare could not finish before the turtle. Learning to trust is like that—slow and steady wins the race.

Once you begin to regain trust in others, then you may let your heart take some risks, maybe reaching out to others in relationships that can be establishing friendships, restoring family relationships, or simply being around people again. It may be telling people about what happened to you without all the details. It may even be as bold as forgiving the person who hurt you. Only you know what you need to feel healed. It will be a slow process, but like the turtle, slow and steady wins the race. Remember this, there is no timeline. It is a process and it could take a lifetime. The one thing I ask is stay true to yourself. Don't give up, don't give in. You will make it through this.

Remember, without spoiling the ending for you, everything is going to be okay.

Kemberlie Sanderson is the executive director of the Crescent House Children's Advocacy Center in Macon, Georgia.

CHAPTER 22

Here's to You, Anne and Lou: Personal Tragedy, Navigating Grief, and Experiencing Triumph and Focused Healing

The more we learn about grief and the damaging waves surrounding abuse, the more it becomes apparent how close these two experiences are deeply related.

Life can be difficult to control sometimes. There seems to be an instinctual urge for most of us to maintain control over the things that may impact our lives in some way. Actions of others that are abusive can be tremendously damaging to the primal mechanism to control. Navigating the winding roads and uncertain paths of life can be a daunting experience. One thing is for certain, each person will experience a trauma at some point in his or her life. Controlling how one responds to the many trials life may throw will have a lasting impact and focus the outcome of every situation.

Personal Tragedy:

Overcoming personal tragedies is best demonstrated at a Children's Advocacy Center not only for the hundreds of children that it serves each year but on a deeper more personal level. This particular advocacy center had some unique experiences in one year that helped to prepare the staff for major life moments, catastrophe, and triumph.

The Child Advocacy Center is located in Columbus, Georgia, which is the second largest metropolitan city in the state. The small staff of two young employees serves more than 350 child victims of abuse, neglect, and maltreatment. There are no two cases that are the same; each requires a tailored approach that is child focused. People often ask them, "How can you all do what you do?" and the response invariably is, "How can we not?" When a child walks through the doors, broken, scared, and hopeless, it is an inherent duty to respond. Often times, a response to the situation derives from personal experiences with tragedy and trauma. No better example than the inspiring year they faced in 2015.

June 22, 2015 is the day that everything started to change. It is the day that our victim advocate started her job at the CAC and embarked on a new journey of sharing hope and healing for victims of abuse. It is also the day that her world stood still. It is the exact day that her father left this

> "One thing is for certain, each person will experience a trauma at some point in his or her life. Controlling how one responds to the many trials life may throw will have a lasting impact and focus the outcome of every situation."

earth. Her whole world was shattered in an instant, and time seemed to stand still. Yet, there were people moving about their day unaware of the immense pain she experienced. She was left feeling lost, hopeless, and frightened—much like the children she would soon be helping along through their own journey. Picking up the pieces and moving forward from such devastation was something that came through much support of those around her and an internal strength fueled by her desire to pour her heart into the lives of others.

Flash forward to September 26, 2015 and the CAC had experienced yet another devastating tragedy when the director's mother passed away after a courageous battle with cancer. Once again, there was another employee with a tremendous blow to her sense of security that left her feeling lost and alone. It was hard to make sense of all of the pain that these two people were experiencing within three months of one another. It was in this moment, an unimaginable pain set in, a gut-wrenching pain that is so deeply seeded and shadowed with the darkness of hopelessness. Once again, we faced the same emotions as we had months before that reminded us of the child victims that we served. The overwhelming feeling of hopelessness and tragedy was something that we had seen each day at the CAC and in the faces of the children we served.

It is not our suggestion that losing someone you love is the same as experience of being abused. However, death and abuse are both tragic and traumatic experiences. Both are deeply painful, personal, and emotional. Both elicit a physical and raw response that is reflective of how a person is equipped to handle these situations.

Navigating Grief and Experiencing Triumph:

Some mental health experts have compared survivors of abuse to those who experience grief. There is a definite sense of loss in both situations: a loss of innocence, a loss of a cherished relationship, and even a loss of control. Grief and traumatic stress can manifest physically, and it is vital that one is aware of the damaging patterns that may present as a result of limited coping abilities. It is vital to acknowledge WHAT the loss is that one is experiencing in order to move forward toward healing.

Grief can be a selfish process, and for survivors of abuse, this can be a difficult concept to come to terms with. Much like the women at the CAC, survivors of abuse have to operate from moment to moment and then day to day in the initial stages. There were days early in the process where they did not want to get out of bed and come to work. There's a period of avoidance that is normal. Sometimes that is the only way to move forward for the moment, to pretend. It was easy to pretend that she could call her mother or stop by her father's house in the afternoon simply to get through the day. This is common with survivors as well; it is easy to pretend that the situation did not happen or that this person that you once loved could not / did not ever betray your trust. This behavior is acceptable for a while but certainly not helpful long term. It's important to remain aware of your own personal strategies for coping while acknowledging the reality of the situation. Often times this is achieved safely with the help of a counselor or therapist. Much like a forensic interview, any time a neutral unbiased party is involved there is ample time for self-refection and a purposeful organization of thoughts and feelings.

Focused Healing:

One of the most important components of healing for the women was sharing their pain with one another. Not just the I-don't-feel-well-today type of pain; the deep, guttural, knife-twisting pain that made the air thick and difficult to breathe. The raw emotions connected to grief and trauma had to come to the surface. One night they were preparing for a conference they were hosting the next day. Both were running on empty and extremely exhausted as they were going on a thirteen-hour work day. They had several items left to purchase from the store; begrudgingly they set out on their journey to finalize the last of the tasks. Suddenly, without warning a song came over the radio, and like a tidal wave of emotion, both were overcome with deep sadness. Tears released from their tired eyes and they began to feel the sudden emptiness and loneliness that seemed to have come out of nowhere. It was then that they realized this must be how child victims feel when they have flashbacks or bursts of emotions that are unexplained. It is not uncommon for children who experience trauma or abuse to lash out at others, to cry unexpectedly, have nightmares, or lack the ability to control their emotions. This is because the child's brain is simply trying to make sense of the situation and regulating emotions can become quite tricky. Physical pain can also be used as a deflection for emotional pain, which largely presents in self-destructive behaviors like cutting or self-harming. It is important to seek professional help if you are experiencing any of these symptoms. Having someone to assist in navigating the difficult emotions and behaviors can help to identifying healthier coping strategies.

The true testament to overcoming tragedy was evidenced by the ability of the two women to bond together and focus their energy on assisting others through their own experience and journey. Often times in the midst of tragedy we are left asking why or what now. Moving forward and finding ways to keep living is especially difficult.

Picking up the pieces or finding ways to keep on moving can be a challenge. Many people discover a strength buried deep within, others use faith, and others cope by trying to make sense of everything with a purposeful meaning. For the two women at the Children's Advocacy Center, interacting with and hearing the brave survivors' experiences and seeing how courageous each child was served as a reminder of their purpose to assist others experiencing trauma.

Someone once said it is easier to raise healthy children than repair broken adults. It is vital for a child who experienced a traumatic event to have an outlet for emotional expression and to feel supported, no matter how big or small. A child's sense of security is mainly comprised of the individuals in their lives that love and care for them. They too must be aware of the sensitive nature of child trauma.

Whether you are sitting in the hills of the Blue Ridge Mountains or off the coast of the Golden Isle or even right here down the banks of the Chattahoochee River in Columbus, you have a team rooting for you—a team that knows how courageous you are, a team that firmly believes that no matter what has happened to you it does not hold the power to define you, to limit you or control your life. See, we advocates believe you possess that power; you can and will conquer trauma, tragedy, and loss. It will not be an easy road, but you are not alone. Even if we might be grieving over the loss of a beloved parent or the loss of innocence, we share a unique and special bond. The bonds we share are filled with pain and sorrow, but with the support from each other we can use this pain and turn it into purpose. Every experience we have shapes the path of our lives. We must make a choice when faced with unimaginable pain, a choice to either give up or become triumphant.

Take your time. Healing is a process and is different for each person. You may stumble on your journey to healing from the pain, but pick up and carry on. Find strength within yourself and from those who support you, both near and far. Take it from us, encouragement can be found all around whether it's from the eyes of a precious child here at the Child Advocacy Center or the ever-steadfast love of an angel.

Even when you feel like all hope is lost, know that there is someone cheering for you.

So here's to you, Anne and Lou.

Samantha DeFranks is the director and Kalen Sieck is the forensic services specialist at the Children's Tree House in Columbus, Georgia.

CHAPTER 23

A New Life, A New Beginning

To the child or children: Any amount of child abuse can have a lasting impact on the child affected, as well as their family, both immediate and extended. It is one of the most awful things that could happen to someone, especially a child. It does not matter the age, race, sex, or background. It does not matter if the child is from lower class, middle class, or upper class; it affects all to some degree. Though these things happen, this does not mean it is the end; a child can still go on to be great and do great things. Life does go on. It may not seem this way at first, but rest assured, it does. Sometimes forgiving happens quickly and sometimes it takes a little bit longer. But life does go on, and the child and their families can be whole again. It does not mean this is the end.

Abuse affects every aspect of a child as well as their families. It takes away the safety, security, self-esteem, and self-confidence of the child and causes the family to doubt everything else from that point forward. A child is something precious and represents everything that is right in this world. When that innocence is taken away, it can be hard to come back around, but you can come back from it.

What happens to these children is not their fault nor is it always the fault of the parents and their families. It may feel that way but that could not be farther from the truth. As parents, we would like to say that we keep our kids safe, but all we can do is try and teach them how things are supposed to be. We cannot watch our kids every second of every day. Sometimes bad things happen that we, as parents, have no control over. But we can teach our kids how to come back and overcome something like this.

When abuse happens, a very large part of the child is taken away; however, they can get that part of themselves back. They do not have to be broken forever, only for now. They may not be who they were originally supposed to be, but they can be a better version of who they would have been. There is no rhyme or reason why these things happen, but they do happen nonetheless. It is not because the child deserved this, rather it is because the person who did this to them could not see their true worth. A child is not an object but a smaller version of a person. A child is not to be thrown away like an old toy. A child is to be embraced by those they love and themselves. Though they may be damaged by this abuse, they are not all together discarded. They should be taken care of and molded into a fine young adult with great potential!

> *"Family, what a powerful word. Your family does not have to just be your immediate family. Family can be your church, your friends, those that have been through the same experiences. It is this extended family that can help you overcome this and it is this family that can be your solid ground upon which to build a newer and stronger foundation for you."*

It is an evil thing when abuse happens to a child. This does not mean that the child has to be defined by this evil; rather they can be made new again! Just remember, it does take work and time to do this. The healing does not occur overnight, rather it occurs over time. But rest assured, little ones, healing does happen and you can come back from this and be a stronger, better version of you. These evil things never truly go away; they just become a part of who you were and who you will be but that does not mean it has to handicap you. It will haunt you and you will always wonder why, but sometimes there are no answers as to the why this happens. You cannot control how it affects you, but you can control what you do with this hurt. Who you become is not who you were but merely an upgraded version of yourself.

But like many other things, you have to let the healing process run its course. Never forget what you went through and use it to make yourself better and use it to help others either directly or through the telling of your experiences. This is not the end; it is only a new beginning. It is not your fault, only the fault of the person(s) that did this to you. Do not think of it as being chosen because of your weaknesses; rather, you were chosen because you can get through it and help others. You will get through it and you will get over this hurdle. Life is full of hurdles and obstacles but they are all meant to be overcome. You can overcome this and you will survive; life goes on, it just takes a different and better path.

How does life go on? Well, put simply, it does. Your life will be different. That does not mean it has to be worse nor does it mean you have to feel worthless; taken advantage of, yes, but only in the moments that those things happened to you. Do not let the abuse you experienced define who you are, who you will love, who you will trust, or how successful you will be. You wonder how can you love again, how can you trust again? Well, the answer is simple: what happened to you was done by one person or a couple of people, but not all people are the same as the one(s) who hurt you. Will it be harder to love? Yes. Will it be harder to trust? Yes. But you can love again and you can trust again. Do not let this one person(s) decide how you see everyone else because not everyone else did this to you; only the one(s) who hurt you.

The world is full of children that this has happened to, and the world is full of children who overcame this abuse and became happy teenagers and adults again. You were meant for greatness, so do not let this one moment in time take that greatness away from you; this person(s) who hurt you has taken enough away from you, but they have not taken away all of you, only a portion of the person you were. Be the person you want to be and the person you should be. Empower yourself with the fact that you survived this and overcame the abuse. You have a strength about you that most adults do not and cannot hope to have, ever. You have survived the worst of the worst, and though you did not come through it unscathed, you did come through it. The emotional scars will always be there but it does not mean these scars have to control you. Take control of this anguish and pain and be great.

Know that you are special, know that people care about you and love you. Know that this is not the end, just another chapter in the book called your life. You are beautiful and unique and handsome and strong, and your strength is projected out into the world. This strength is what defines you, not the abuse you were subjected to at the hands of someone you trusted and loved. This strength is what you tap into to get through and overcome this. This strength is what will make you able to love again and trust again. This strength is a strength that very few can claim to have. Know that you have this strength and be proud of the person you are and the person you have yet to become. This strength is your spirit that is unique and special to only you. You may be a little damaged, but you are not broken! That is how we know you will get through this. There is light at the end of the tunnel for you and your families.

To the families: This is something that affects you all as well. It is a very traumatic and trying time for you all. But like your child, you will get through it individually and together and you will be stronger than you ever were, and the bonds you form as a result of this will be unbreakable. It is important for the family to know that what happened was no one's fault but the person(s) who did this. A parent cannot beat themselves up for letting this happen. You did not let this happen; it just happened. You could not have done anything differently, so please do not beat yourselves up for it. It is not the child's fault and it is not your fault. Never lose hope and faith in your child or yourself; like your child you will weather this storm too. This is not the end; it is only a new beginning. Do not let this define you and do not blame yourself. Parents, you cannot get stuck it the "what ifs" and the "what could have been." Regroup and reform and be the best you can be. Life goes on!

What's done is done, but you cannot let it consume you or you will lose even more of those precious moments. Not only do you have to be strong for your child but you have to be strong for your family and yourself. You too have to overcome this and you will, but like your child, it will take time. It may take longer or it may not take that long at all, but you will get past this. You may not be the kind of normal you were, but you can still be normal and you can still thrive as a family. None of you can do it alone, just remember there are people who love you and care for you that can be your saving grace. Love each other, care for each other, and support one another; that is how you will get through this. You will get through this. It may not seem like things will ever be the same again and they may not be, but you can redefine what that means. The night is always darkest before the dawn; however, the sun will shine on you and your family again. Know this and you will be an unstoppable force and a beacon of hope for those in need. You can share your experiences, and by doing so you may be another's saving grace. Use this unspeakable act to pave a new way for you and your family and others that may be in need.

YOU WILL GET THROUGH THIS! You are not alone! There are others who have been through similar incidents and there are others who have gotten through it as well. You may feel alone on this journey, but rest assured, you are not! Someone is always watching over you. There is always someone who can share in your pain and in your healing. This is not the end; just a new beginning. You may have momentarily lost hope, but never lose faith. Never lose faith in your child, your family, and yourself. Because at the end of the day, family is all you truly have.

Family, what a powerful word. Your family does not have to just be your immediate family. Family can be your church, your friends, those that have been through the same experiences. It is this extended family that can help you overcome this and it is this family that can be your solid ground upon which to build a newer and stronger foundation for you. You are not alone in this struggle. Is it a constant battle? Yes, but it is one that you can and will win. You will be victorious. You do not have to go quietly into the night. Be the sounding board and set the standard for others to follow. By doing this, you will create greatness within yourself and within your family. You can and will be a beacon of hope for those that have not yet had to endure this degree of evil. You can do this because you are strong enough to. You can do this because you are now soldiers and you must never quit and never give up. You must fight and you must continue the fight; and you will because you have the strength to do just that.

To the child or children and the family: It may seem like the world has closed in on you, but that is not the case. Your world is yours for the shaping. This new world of yours is scary, but you have the power to overcome this fear. The strength you have may be unknown or untapped, but it is there nonetheless. Tap into this strength and forge a new world for you, your child, and your family. You can make a new life and you can have a new beginning—you deserve it!

Lt. KB Ayers, director, and Sgt. Adam Blanks work for the Monroe County Sheriff's Office's C.A.R.E. Cottage in Forsyth, Georgia.

CHAPTER 24

#GOFIGHTWIN

It's the fourth quarter and your team is down by a few points. As the team gets in formation, the battle cry of "**GO** big blue! **FIGHT** to **WIN!**" Then "**GO, FIGHT, WIN!**" The ball is thrown and . . .

This is the drill for every great sport. No matter if it's football, soccer, baseball, no matter what state, country, or world you live in, the chant of empowering a team to win is as essential as apples to an apple pie.

GO . . . FIGHT . . . WIN!

I want you to stand or sit where you can see your reflection; it can be a mirror or simply before you boot-up your computer. I just want you to see yourself in the last quarter of any sport you choose. Now, it's up to you to bring the win home for your team. I want you to feel the excitement and the intensity of the crowd and the adrenaline pumping through your body. **HOLD IT!**

Now, hear the battle cry. **GO! FIGHT! WIN!** Keep repeating this until it becomes a medley in your head.

GO!
Go and be beautiful . . .
Go and be smart . . .
Go and be resilient . . .
Go and be large . . .Go and finish and never stop!

FIGHT!
Fight till it hurts . . .
Fight your doubts . . .
Fight your critics . . .
Fight the voices . . .

WIN!
Win over the situation . . .
Win over the critics . . .
Win over the voices . . .
Win over the self-doubt . . .
Win over . . . Win over . . . Win over!

As your imagination starts to fade, remember the chant of the battle cry of **GO! FIGHT! WIN!**

Remember the moments when your team won, or when you were part of the crowd cheering their team to victory. Live in this moment; seize the memory and capture that space.

Within that space is where I want you to chant your battle cry. When the world just seems so unfair or just plain cruel, find this space and say softly, **Go! Fight! Win!** Then keep increasing in volume and intensity until you are there. You are in whatever arena in whatever state or country in whatever sport you choose. You are surrounded by a relentless energy of empowerment. You feel the words pulsating through your body. It started in your toes and moved through your feet. It's moving up your leg and reached the pit of your stomach. You tremble a little but you totally have control. As it moves through your chest, you hear your heartbeat, you still have control. Now it moves through your arms and fingers; again, you have control. As it moves through your ears and eyes, you have a focus that you have never felt before, things are clearer and crisper. You know that you are ready. You have all the control. You are the champion of your destiny. You are the winner over this moment. *GO, FIGHT, to WIN.*

Now, as the dust settles and the crowds begin to scatter, and you are standing/sitting there staring into the empty stands, I want you to read this letter. This is the letter to a stronger you. Just like life's opportunities, this letter is endless. Read it once you can't hear the chant (Go! Fight! Win!) Read this when you need a hoorah, or just read this as an affirmation to how far you have come and to the endless places you will go.

To: A Stronger Me

Hello Friend,

It's been a journey—some rough roads and some wrong detours, but through it all you are here.
Maybe a little more doubtful, maybe a little less angry, maybe just plain confused at times. But you are here . . .
Here to laugh,
Here to cry,
Here to get mad, and
Here to ask why?

Regardless of the journey, it was yours to take, and although you might not know it, it is yours to make.

You are stronger than you could ever imagine, and with that strength you have a story to tell; and with that strength you have a mission to complete; and with that strength you will find a quiet peace.

This journey through life is what it is. No promises of roses, no promises of perfection; just promises of life. And whatever that looks like for you, it is your life to own, so own it! Give it all you've got. Dig deep and plant your soul in it. This is and always can be the first day of the rest of your life.

So, when you feel as if no one understands, they do.
When you feel as if no one cares, they do.
When you feel that the world is against you, it is not.
When you feel that you are alone, you are not.
When you want to laugh but you can't, you can.
When you want to scream to the top of your voice, do it.
When you feel as if all hope is gone, it is not.

You are stronger than that moment. Each day brings you strength, each strength gives you hope, each hope gives you life, and with that life just live.

From: A Stronger You

Sabrina Callaway is the former director at the Rainbow House Connections Child Advocacy and Assessment Center in Jonesboro, Georgia, and also a forensic interviewer.

ABOUT THE CHILDREN'S ADVOCACY CENTERS OF GEORGIA

The Children's Advocacy Centers of Georgia (CACGA) is a statewide membership organization of children's advocacy centers all across Georgia. CACGA was incorporated in 1994 and was one of the first state chapters in the nation. CACGA now includes forty-six Children's Advocacy Centers providing services to more than 8,000 children each year.

A children's advocacy center is designed to provide a child-friendly and safe environment in which CAC professionals can meet with law enforcement and child protective service investigators to conduct and observe the forensic interviews of children who have alleged sexual abuse, physical abuse, neglect, and/or exploitation. CACs are also designed to reduce the trauma to child victims by bringing multidisciplinary team (MDT) members together at the CAC to share information and therefore reduce the need for duplicative services. Our MDT members include not just law enforcement and child protective services, but prosecution, medical professionals, family and victim advocates, and mental health professionals. As such, each case is reviewed from the date of a child's disclosure of alleged abuse and continues through investigation, medical and mental health treatment, and prosecution.

On behalf of the Children's Advocacy Centers of Georgia and the hundreds of dedicated and caring professionals who within our forty-six CACs, thank you for reading this book, and thank you for supporting children and families – and your Children's Advocacy Center -- in your communities.

For more information, please visit us online at www.cacga.org.

Edwards Brothers Malloy
Ann Arbor MI. USA
June 19, 2017